# Leading High Performers

# Praise for Leading High Performers

*"A very insightful guide for leaders of all disciplines. Eric Snow speaks from the experience of leading some of the best in the game. There should be a copy of this book in every book shelf."* -- **Danny Lanier, Leadership Coach, Former Financial Executive Lucent Technologies and AT&T**

*"Growing up in Michigan I was able to follow Eric and his outstanding career. I have always associated Eric and the word leader as one in the same. Not only did he get the most out of his talent, he inspired his teammates to do the same. Eric is a true warrior! A captain who kept the ship steady."* - **Chris Webber, NBA Great and Commentator TNT**

*"When you're the starting point guard for two teams that make it to the NBA finals, selected Captain of your teams for numerous years, it shows you sweat and bleed leadership. Eric Snow developed his natural leadership abilities to become a nationally respected role model on and off the court."* -- **Steve Smith, NBA Veteran and Olympic Gold Medal Winner**

*"Eric has truly been a great leader and friend throughout his years in the NBA. I was a teammate on the 76ers with Eric for about 4 years in which he helped me grow as a player and become and All Star under his leadership. Eric was brought into a team of young hungry ballers with the biggest name in basketball at the time Allen Iverson. Although Allen was the star Eric using his leadership qualities managed Allen's expectations and was the glue to the growth of the 76ers making it to the 2001 finals.*

*Simply put, we don't make the NBA Finals or upset the eventual champion L.A. Lakers in Game 1 without Eric guiding us as our leader and helping us reach our best.*

*That is what Eric has been doing for all of his career. He helps us all be our very best"* -- **Theo Ratliff, former teammate, Philadelphia 76ers**

# Leading High Performers:

*The Ultimate Guide to Being a*
**Fast**, **Fluid** *and* **Flexible** *Leader*

## By Eric Snow

Foreword by **Ambassador Andrew Young**

Afterword by **Bishop Eddie Long**

New York

# Leading High Performers
## The Ultimate Guide to Being a Fast, Fluid, and Flexible Leader

Cover Design by:  Rachel Lopez
            Rachel@r2cdesign

ISBN 978-1-60037-718-1

Library of Congress Control Number: 2009937703

# MORGAN · JAMES
**THE ENTREPRENEURIAL PUBLISHER**

Morgan James Publishing
1225 Franklin Ave., STE 325
Garden City, NY 11530-1693
Toll Free 800-485-4943
www.MorganJamesPublishing.com

In an effort to support local communities, raise awareness and funds, Morgan James Publishing donates one percent of all book sales for the life of each book to Habitat for Humanity. Get involved today, visit **www.HelpHabitatForHumanity.org.**

# Acknowledgements

This may have been the most difficult part of the book to write. How do you thank all the people who have helped make you who you are? So many special people contributed to this book – and my life. I'd like to mention just a few by name:

My parents, Hubert and Susie Snow – You both have been my lifetime guides. You made every doubtful thing look hopeful. I am a product of your love and work ethic. Because of you, I always believed I could attain anything.

My brothers and sisters (Shirley, Patrick, Ricky, Betty, Percy, Linda) – At every stage in my life, I knew I had six people who would support me, back me and do anything to help me become a better person. Thank you for expecting me to do right.

Extended family and friends – Thank you for your love and support. It's a great feeling to know that you always have your family with you. Each of you knows who you are and how you've touched my life. You are a blessing from God.

Every coach I've ever had – How can you lead without a great example to follow? Thanks for helping develop me personally and professionally. Each of you contributed to who I am as a player and a person.

Teammates – My high school, college and NBA teammates have made a permanent mark on my life. I will never forget any of you and how you've changed me. Thank you.

The City of Canton, Ohio - Thanks for your support throughout the years. What a great city! No matter where I live, Canton will always be home!

Michigan State University – Thank you for supporting my family and me throughout my career. MSU will always hold a special place in my heart.

My fans - Without you, I never would have heard my name from the stands. Your cheers keep me going.

Book contributors - Thank you to Raoul Davis and the entire Ascendant Strategy team and Sheri Riley of Glue, Inc. for your support. Thank you to all of my contributors from Keytura, Inc., who started this process with me and helped bring this idea to life. A special thanks to my representatives Julani Ghana and Steve Kauffman. Your guidance and help have been invaluable.

Thanks also to Amanda Mercado-Petrak, the Cavaliers' PR Representative.

Bishop Eddie L. Long – You have been a great inspiration in my life. I met you as an adult, but the special bond we share makes me feel like you've been there forever, motivating me and being a blessing in my life. Thank you.

Ambassador Andrew Young – You have had a tremendous effect on my life. Because of the ideas you stood up for, I am able to do what I do today. Thank you for sharing your time and wisdom with me.

My family - My wife, DeShawn and sons my Eric ("EJ"), Darius and Jarren. Thank you all for helping me become a better person. Your encouragement, compassion, love, and support mean so much to me. I love you all with a passion!

God – I thank You for being my Savior, and for your grace and mercy.

# Table of Contents

# Foreword by Ambassador Andrew Young

The most important person on any team is the one who finds a way to make those around him perform better. Every team – whether basketball, football, business or non-profit – has the challenge to create a focused force toward its objectives. Almost any team, especially a sports team, is subject to the influence of egos. I remember even Dr. Martin Luther King, Jr. describing his staff as a team of wild horses that just happened to be chained together by the Civil Rights Movement. He said each one was constantly trying to pull the team in his or her own direction. The challenge of his leadership and the challenge of the "point guard" – even in the Civil Rights Movement – was to find ways to draw people towards a common objective.

Some people, however, confuse managers with leaders. Managers work according to a business plan, typically giving orders and telling other people what to do. Leaders help you to do what you need to do in order to fulfill your own potential while simultaneously impacting the core competence of the overall team. But here is the tricky thing. No matter how effective a manager' orders are, nothing substantial is ever really achieved until people buy into a vision and realize that their own potential can only be fulfilled as the potential of others around them is filled. This is what leaders do. Managers operate from an authoritarian perspective in a top down fashion. Leaders help people mold their own ego needs into a collective commitment.

Coaches, political leaders and other players often resort to screaming, shouting and cursing in an effort to get people into line. Eric Snow, by his very quiet and positive demeanor, belies that type of leadership. In his roles at both Michigan State and with the Cleveland Cavaliers, he has always been a quiet force that drew men to a common purpose by the magnetism of his ideas and personality. Is this talent one that we're born with, or can it be learned? My contention is that leaders are made by those around them, and none of us are born leaders.

By virtue of his intelligence, his sensitivity, and his ability to put himself in the other person's shoes, Snow has been able to help players from Shawn Respert to LeBron James to perform their best as part of a team. This is critical, and the impact of not encouraging others to work as a group can be seen in the way that Cleveland began to suffer as a team when Snow retired. The team began to rely too much on the phenomenal abilities of its key performers. The problem with that strategy is that great individuals seldom win championships – great teams do. This same concept can be applied to members of any organization, regardless of the type. The leadership model that Eric Snow represents is vital in many arenas: sports leadership, family leadership, and school leadership to name a few.

I remember reading something more than 55 years ago when I was 20 years old. It was a paragraph that led me to embrace this kind of leadership and to try my best to be this type of leader in the Civil Rights Movement and throughout my careers in congress, as mayor and as an ambassador. That passage suggested that teams must strive to find a common commitment, a common ground, and a common vision which magnetically draws each of the individual visions together. "Point guards" can do that as floor managers – basically they are managing the game – but they become leaders when they no longer just distribute the ball, but move the ball to the open man.

That makes the message of this book important for all leaders – not just those who excel in sports. The "open man" could also be the best salesman or the best student. Even in the family setting there are certain things that one child does better than others. There are certain functions that aunts, uncles, family friends and relatives can perform for a child that it's impossible for one person to do alone.

I think that anybody can spend a lifetime learning about leadership and still miss something. It's just that important to explore. There are leadership models that are based on fear, and there are leadership models that are based on love – bringing forth someone's confidence and helping him to become sensitive to the individual and emotional needs of those around them. *Leading High Performers* is based on love – and that's what makes this a book you'll want to read, re-read and build into the way you lead your "team."

# Introduction

It always intrigues me when people ask me how I did it. Sometimes they ask how I've kept my head about me throughout my years in the NBA, how I've remained a strong family man, and how I've stayed true to my morals and values.

The answer is really pretty simple. Being a professional basketball player was not my life goal. Being a leader in all aspects of my life was my ultimate goal.

Now, I will tell you all the things *I think* it takes to be a good leader: things like being a great listener, walking your talk, inspiring others – all the things you've heard a thousand times before and read in a hundred different books. To me, those are just words.

**You could earn a Ph.D. in all these areas and *still* not be a great leader – or even a *good* one, for that matter.**

Here's what really makes a truly great leader: *experience.* Leadership is the process you go through in reaching a personal goal, then reaching out to help *other* people achieve *their* goals, too. In fact, the characteristics that speak volumes to me in the leaders I work with are:

1. A track record of success

2. Genuine concern about my success

3. The ability to get their *own* agendas out of the way

The bottom line is that leaders must care about others. *Great* leaders care deeply about the success of the people around them and of those they help – *without involving their own agendas. True* caring from a leader builds trust; and trust is a key component in any leadership role. If a leader can't be trusted, he won't be followed.

Some people talk about how leaders can *create* trust within their team. There are lots of "strategies" and "techniques" people try to use to create that trust. For example, if I feel that my coach has some hidden agenda behind his interest in me, I am not going to fully receive his advice and coaching. That's just a natural response. When my basketball coach lets go of his own agenda and meets the players with only the *team's* agenda in mind, then I trust that coach 100%. I will take every bit of advice, wisdom and coaching that he can give me – and even ask for more. Why? Because I know that everything he does is to make *me* better, to make *the team* better, and to get the team closer to reaching our *team goals.*

**Trust is a natural response when you know that your leader does not bring his or her personal agenda to the table.**

But trust isn't all you need. A great leader also has to care. In fact, you need to *passionately* care about each and every person that you lead. For a lot of us, true caring can be a very scary thing.

Every child is born a caring individual. Every child cries heartbroken tears of disappointment for him or herself – or for a loved one – when something sad or frightening happens. But, as you grow up and life happens, you learn to protect yourself from this kind of heartbreak. And the more painful your childhood was, the more protective of yourself you become. We build walls to keep from caring too much. We become cold instead of passionate.

Therein is one of the secrets of great leaders. They have reconnected with their passion and with the ability to care. Great leaders are utterly committed to being passionate. It doesn't matter what they do –

coaching the NBA, teaching elementary school or managing a sales force – if they care about it and the people that they work with, then they will be good leaders.

If they have all that and they've already been through the trenches and come out victorious on the other side as successes in their fields, *then they will be great leaders.* And here's the really awesome thing about becoming a leader: Anyone can be a great one. No matter your background, family history or education level, the seeds of leadership are planted the moment you begin care about something deeply enough to "become children" again.

When you become willing to do anything to grow into the person that you need to be in order to obtain what you are passionate about, including letting go of your past and digging deep to connect with your emotions, the leadership ability that lives inside every human being sparks into life. In *that* precise moment, you are a leader.

First, you must learn to lead *yourself* to greatness, whatever that means to you. Greatness can mean anything from discovering the cure for cancer to being the best second-grade teacher you can be. After leading yourself to greatness, you can easily lead others to their greatness. When you become great, it shines through you and will attact others to you.

**Leaders inspire everyone they meet to move toward greatness.**

Great leaders make the world a better place simply by moving through it. Their dedication to reaching higher, further and longer shines in every thing they do – from leading a team to win a crucial game or parenting their children. Leadership isn't something that you *do*. It is what you *are*.

Leadership isn't something special. It's inside of all of us. It's a function of a caring heart and maturity. We are all leaders in our own lives. When you do something well and then reach out to help someone who wants to learn from you, you are leading. When a friend asks for advice and you give it, you are leading. When you talk to the woman in the line at the grocery store, ask for directions, or react with calm in front of your children as someone cuts you off on the freeway, you are leading.

In talking about leadership in this book, we focus on leading high performers.

Whether you've just got promoted to middle management or the new guy in the board room, *Leading High Performers* is no easy feat. I can testify to that, for nearly all of my 14 years in the NBA I was either co-captain or held some leadership role for the teams I was on.

I have a unique understanding of leadership from the blisteringly fast-paced world of professional sports as well as my post-retirement "trial by fire" initiation into the world of instant entrepreneur, investor and businessman. That's why this book is called **Leading High Performers:** *The Ultimate Guide to Being a **Fast**, **Fluid** and **Flexible** Leader.*

I know how it is to be the new guy on the team, thrust into leadership the first day on the job and charged with leading legends of the game and current greats like LeBron James and Allen Iverson. It's not as simple as pointing in the right direction and expecting everyone to follow with a high-five and no ulterior motives.

High performers have high expectations, high skill levels and, frankly, high egos that must be catered to rather than ignored; it can be a job within a job leading high performers to winning results and woe to those who are unprepared.

High performers can be merciless about those they feel are inadequately prepared to lead them; without your high performers you can't get YOUR job done, let alone THE job done. No matter how good you are at what you do, when it comes to high performers you must always be just a little bit better – and when you're not they'll know it, and shut you down.

Unfortunately, there is no cookie-cutter template for leading. However, thanks to fourteen years in the NBA leading among these true giants of the game – and being led by such giants as Michigan State University head coach Tom Izzo and NBA great head coach Larry

Brown – I've developed a plan for staying on your toes when leading and developing high performers.

This plan requires that leaders be *Fast, Fluid and Flexible;* in other words, high performers demand that you be:

- **Fast**: You must learn to respond to high performers immediately; hesitancy is a leadership killer. High performers respond to quick thinkers, decisive decision makers and unwavering confidence; they react negatively to plodders, hesitancy and indecisiveness, often with disastrous results. To help build these skills Eric will share with readers his **4 Pillars of Leading among Giants**.

- **Fluid**: To be fluid is to keep moving the partnership forward regardless of difficulties, challenges, interruptions or obstacles. Fluid leaders respond to crises as they arise but also are committed to preventing crises through continued success. When you are fluid you don't just "go with the flow". You literally **create the flow** regardless of who you are leading. There is nothing high performers respect more than progress – especially when someone else is the architect. To increase the fluid nature of your leadership skills, Eric shares his **6 P's of Leadership Potential** in this section.

- **Flexible**: Finally, you must be flexible. Too many leaders think that ruling with an iron hand is the best way to hammer down their followers, or that stubbornness equals decisiveness. Unfortunately, most high performers will not respond to heavy-handed leadership. Very rarely will you come out on top in a war of egos with a high performer. Instead, they need a leader who can respond to any situation and can create effective solutions to joint problems in a moment's notice. To help you become flexible when dealing with high performers, Eric will share in Part 3 how to **Play All Positions**.

With these three tools, you can lead high performers and produce results. You can also personalize your leadership lessons to create lasting relationships for high-level performance, even under the most demanding circumstances.

What's more, you will be prepared regardless of the economy, the high performer, the task or the company for which you work; the *Fast, Fluid and Flexible* rules work anywhere, every time, for every high performer. Why? Because they don't rely on scripts or cookie cutter templates. Instead, they help you become the best performer possible so that you will be able to lead your high performers more effectively. In other words, regardless of who you are leading, these techniques put the focus squarely on you by creating positive habits that become instinctual the more you use them. They are also highly transferable and will continue to serve you as you assume positions with even greater responsibility.

### Every Leader Needs Mentors

I have made the effort to learn from and be mentored by some of the greatest leaders in sports and in the world. I consider myself a great leader when my team votes me team captain or when my wife trusts me to listen to her and give solid advice, or when my children come to me with their problems. But mostly I consider myself a great leader because I am happy with the way my life has worked out. If people can't lead themselves to their own personal best, then they're not qualified to lead anyone else.

#### If you can't do it for you, what makes you think that you can do it for anyone else?

On those early mornings back in college when I got myself up and out of bed and out to the track – despite being tired and sore – I learned how to lead myself. Leadership starts in your heart in those moments that no one else sees and with those things you tell yourself that no one else hears.

You see, I've never *sought out* leadership positions. When I deserved them, they came to me. When I didn't, they didn't. It was that simple. I was with the Philadelphia 76ers the first time my team voted me captain. I was shocked, but I trusted their vision of me, and they trusted me to step up and be a leader.

This book is for all of you who are asked to lead. It's not meant to be a manual – I have nothing to teach you. All I have is what my mentors shared with me along the way and what I've learned from my experiences. This book is simply a collection of my stories, experiences, and sound advice from the encouraging hand of a friend who wants to share the great moments with you – and to help you through the tough times. Within these pages, seven men whom I consider some of the elite leaders in America – and certainly within the game of basketball – offer their candid thoughts on leading others. You'll read thoughts on leadership from:

LeBron James, a teammate in Cleveland;

Daniel Gibson, another teammate in Cleveland;

Allen Iverson, a perennial all-star with the Memphis Grizzlies;

Larry Brown, head coach of the Charlotte Bobcats;

Tom Izzo, head coach at Michigan State University;

Nate McMillan, head coach of the Portland Trail Blazers; and

Jud Heathcote, former head coach at Michigan State University.

They each write about their personal definitions of good and bad leadership, and they name the people who not only shaped their lives but the sport of basketball and the world we live in. I asked each of them the same six questions. Their answers are printed at the end of the chapters with themes that mirror their own views.

# Part 1:

# Running the Point –
# A Revolution in Leadership

# Chapter 1:

## New Times Demand New Leaders

*"No matter what business you're in, you can't run in place or someone will pass you by. It doesn't matter how successful you've been."*

~ **Jim Valvano**

I t's a new world.
And it's time to think of leadership in a new way.

I won't try to pretend that a changing world is a new phenomenon. It isn't. What *is* new is the way change occurs in our world today – *fast*.

Throughout history, humanity has always created new and better ways to live and work as a result of changes in the environment. And today is really no different, except that it doesn't take thousands of years for change to happen and become part of the culture. That happens rapidly today. We may not have to resort to hunting and gathering to make sure our needs are met, but like our early ancestors, our culture today is still marked by a desire to work hard and achieve our goals regardless of changes in our environment. We live in a world where information is literally at our fingertips and accessible twenty four hours a day, and one that is charaterized by rapid change in every area of life. And we have become comfortable with change of this nature. This has created a generation of people who want what they want, when they want it. We work longer and harder, and we expect more from ourselves and those around us. We live in a world where people are expected to move quickly, multi-task effectively, and respond to change without missing a step. Our lives have become much more complex as we find ourselvers not only impacted by what goes on close to home, but also globally.

The way the world thinks about leadership has also changed tremendously over time. And this is to be expected. While some of the basic ideas about what it takes to lead successfully haven't changed at all, the manner in which people lead has changed to meet the demands of the world we live in today.

And what a different world it is.

## The Old Model of Leadership Simply Can't Work Any Longer

When I think of the old model of leadership, I think of hierarchies and top-down management styles where people do what they are told and stay in their place. Leaders are the ones in 'power' who micromanage employees. Employees are expected to 'follow' their leaders, not make any trouble, and just get their jobs done. And this model worked in the past.

But not any longer. We live in a different world, and people are no longer content, or expected, to be worker bees.

Today, the Internet generation's casual, fast-paced, instantly gratified lifestyle requires people to be more agile and think faster and better on their feet. They are masters at multi-tasking. Gone are the days of getting up at 7 am, reporting to work by 8 am, and leaving at 5 pm. A typical employee might get up at 5:30 am for a visit to the gym, is home by 7 am to wake up the kids, gets to work by 8:30 am, works through lunch, puts in 10-12 hours a day when needed, stops by the market on the way home from work or perhaps attends his or her's child's football game, gets dinner on the table while revieiwng homework with the kids, perhaps catches a TV show before bed, and maybe takes a look at their email before finally dropping off to sleep. They cram in a variety of tasks into their work day. They are expected to get their work done under tight deadlines, juggle multiple meetings and commitments, and operate at peak performance. They are expected to be driven, work hard, and still have a persoal life. They work autonomously and want opportunites to contribute and be recognized for their contributions.

So how do we live in a world that demands such flexibility, dedication and drive? Well, for starters, we become leaders in our own lives that recognize that leadership must change with the times. There is a desperate need for solid, effective leadership that works into today's society for today's workers. Why? Because the old models simply aren't working anymore.

People today are full of initiative and crave independence. They have a strong sense of what they can offer and how they can contribute to an organization's goals, and they want to be heard. In short, they are **_high performers_** and expected to contribute greatly. This is drastically different from workplace relationships that were common fewer than fifity years ago that were characterized by compliant, dependant workers. Leaders must change the way they lead the new workforce, and the new workforce of today that consiststs of highly talented and independent minds demands it. Leaders who understand this concept will always be asked to step into additional leadership roles.

To help make this point clearer, let's look at the game of basketball thirty to forty years ago. Nothwithstanding the five men, one ball, wooden floor and two hoops, it bears little resemblance to the game of today. Basketball in the past was very mechanical. Back then, the game was about setting up and executing plays. It was more similar to a chess game than the _be-ready-for-anything style_ of today's play. That system worked back then, and it worked flawlessly Today's game is more fluid and would not work based on the methods of the past. It would be absolutely laughable if a team tried to revert to the more choreographed styles of play of the past.

You can apply this example to leadership as well. And since the game has changed, you will have to change the tools you use.

Here's how.

## The Changing Game of Leadership

For leadership to be effective in today's environment, it must be three things:

**Fast:** Leaders must respond to changes without hesitancy and indeciveness.

**Fluid:** Leaders must keep moving their teams forward regardless of difficulties, challenges, interruptions or obstacles.

**Flexible:** Leaders must be able to respond to any situation and create effective solutions to problems in a moment's notice.

In addition, leaders must implement these three components within a strategy based on a shared *vision* that must instill in each team member a sense of ownership of the goals of the group. This is how you create a championship team. Championship teams, in business or in sports, have one thing in common and it isn't the most talented players or the most charismatic coach. It isn't money or location or luck. *It is a common vision and great respect for that vision.* This commonality creates a shared dedication to improving performance from game to game or project to project.

In true, high-performance teams, it is the sense of ownership and the ability to understand and carry out the game plan that brings success, no matter the personal sacrifice or gain. No longer is it good enough to be great at one skill. It takes ten hands to make a basket on the court and a team to succeed in business. Effective leaders reward team members for their ability to push the collective vision forward more often than rewarding an individual's personal ability to execute a specific task. When a team is structured around a common vision, it creates a sense of integrity that makes the group rock-solid. Each member becomes accountable to the other members of the team and, most importantly, to him or herself. The ability to create a team with this kind of integrity and focus is the key to successfully leading high performance teams into today's business environment.

## Basketball and Business Leadership Today

While I am known as a student of the game of basketball, I'm also a student of the game of life. I also read and study a great deal. And without sounding redundant, I want to share some interesting parallels that can be drawn between basketball and life – and the new leadership style of today.

In today's business environment, basketball and the lessons that can learned by watching and playing the game are often used as a model for effective leadership. Years ago, football was the standard. In football, the coach calls all the plays and each player simply carries out his or her designated role. This is very similar to the typical top-down management style that I mentioned earlier and may have been a great way to teach leadership skills in the pre-Internet age. It simply doesn't work in today's organizations. If a player is injured in a football game, that player is taken out and replaced and the game continues. The strategy itself is not altered.

However, basketball uses 12 player teams, and if a player is injured, the entire strategy is regorganized and now takes into account the change in the team with the loss of the injured player and the addition of the replacement. The vision does not change. The strategy is revised, but the overall goal remains the same – to win. This is exactly what happens in organizations. When key personnel leaves, the organization doesn't stop functioning and the goals do not change. Work continues and people adjust rapidly to change. And this is exactly what it means to be *fast, fluid and flexible*. These concepts describe a model that encourages leaders and those they lead to adapt to change and get the job done.

**When strategy meets flexibility, the result is
the basketball model of leadership.**

Instead of creating a master plan and forcing team members to stick to it regardless of the individual's natural gifts, it is far more effective to create a plan and then devise a flexible strategy that allows everyone to respond to changes in the team and the environment. With all team members operating at full capacity in a game plan that maximizes their talents and skills in a flexible way, it's easy to understand how this method is far more effective, yielding a much higher likelihood of reaching the goal.

The basketball model of business leadership is gaining steam because it combines the best of traditional leadership theory (i.e. structure and strategy) with the leadership concepts that are driven by the way we work today (i.e. being fast, fluid and flexible) into a model that maximizes the potential of both. It's partly because basketball demands a level of leadership that can consistently create teams with both *personal responsibility* and the *autonomy* to make split-second decisions in incredibly high-stakes situations.

In basketball, the team is everything. A solid team that trusts each other, communicates well, and feels a sense of collective responsibility will beat a team of more talented, but less cohesive players. The trick is learning how to establish an environment that will create a team out of competitive, highly-driven individuals. In a recent study titled, *Trust in Lleadership and Team Performance: Evidence from NCAA Basketball*, published in *The Journal of Applied Psychology* in 2000, researchers discovered that trust in leadership is both a product and a determinant of team performance. If the team trusts its leader, the team will be more successful. But what is considered common sense today wasn't common sense even 20 years ago. The old school style of leadership depended more on *fear* than on *trust* to create success. There was an emphasis on *punishment* versus *learning*. Old school coaches tended to be very autocratic and demanded obedience. For example, the whistle that used to be so commonly used in practices is hardly ever used today. Duke University Coach Mike Krzyzewski, arguably one of the most effective coaches in the history of college basketball, refuses to use a whistle. He believes that it creates distance between himself and his players. "Coach K" has been a strong proponent of the importance of trust in effective coaching, and believes a coach must have the player's trust to build an effective working relationship. In his book, *Leading with the Heart*, Coach K states, "Almost everything in leadership comes back to relationships."

A person can create those relationships through high-trust, low-shame interactions with team players; understanding the flexible nature of business and team players today; and creating and effectively communicating the team vision and gaining buy-in from all team players. These action steps combine to create the new leadership style of today.

## Leading High Performers Requires True L.E.A.D.E.R.S.

Before you can be *Fast, Fluid and Flexible*, however, you must first be ready to lead. We begin this book with a simple checklist to make sure you are up to the challenge of *Leading High Performers*:

- **Learn**: First, you must establish that you are still learning and can get better. Be humble enough to accept the ideas of those you lead and new ideas in general. Make it clear that you are not afraid to grow but that you expect those you lead to continue to grow as well. Remind them that they can still get better; frankly, that they have to get better.

- **Evaluate:** Continue to study their strengths and weaknesses. Steer them towards what they do well and minimize their weaknesses until they are prepared to improve them. Put them in a position where their strengths ALWAYS outweigh their weaknesses. You know what they don't do well, you will not allow it to be exploited and, frankly, they will owe you for that.

- **Ambition**: Don't be afraid to shoot too high or reach too far; giants in any game appreciate ambition. High performers love new challenges and want to win. They have an insatiable appetite for success. However, they also have a strong fear of failure. Your job as a leader is to help them focus on their desire to succeed in order to minimize their fear of failure. That is why spending time with your high performers and gaining their trust through open communication is important. Getting to the root of their fear of failure may not be easy, but it is there. All high performers find it hard to lose.

- **Discipline**: Leading by example begins with you, and you will be expected to be an example to those you lead. You must practice what you preach while being firm and consistent. You are an example for those you guide, and they will expect you to model this principle in both actions and words.

- **Endure**: Be prepared to endure criticism that will inevitably come from your work or relationship with the high performer. There will be jealousy, envy and, inevitably, in-fighting. How do you handle criticism? You have to take the high road. You also have to be able to endure criticism from the high performer. They, too, will test you.You will need to find ways to improve but you must be OPEN for conversation and dialogue. "How can you help me?" is a great question for the high performer. Be open for feedback and criticism.

- **Reassure**: Many high performers are amazingly insecure. Oftentimes, the greater the performer, the higher the level of insecurity; some will need constant reinforcement and encouragement. Leaders who display enthusiasm and encouragement will help ensure that success *will* happen and that there will be a payoff. Things can get stale, so a good leader finds ways to motivate or push their high performers while finding their passion. How do you encourage them to keep working and meet their goals? When to push and when not to push are critical skills that are valuable to anyone who leads high performers.

- **Sacrifices**: Leading high performers can require an enormous sacrifice. You must be willing to give up some things to help develop others, even if it means foregoing an immediate reward for yourself (such as a promotion or bonus). High performers make sacrifices, to be sure, but the leader's sacrifice will be greater and often times will be less appreciated.

Now let's move on to some of the leadership myths that are pervasive in our society. I've experienced or encountered many of these in my years as a leader. These are myths or "stories we tell ourselves" that hold us back from our true leadership potential.

# Chapter 2:

## Leadership Myths

*"Never underestimate the power of dreams and the influence of the human spirit. The potential for greatness lives within each of us."*

### ~ Wilma Rudolph

We've all heard the myths, the lies, the rationalizations about leadership that float around:

> "People are *born* leaders – they can't be *made*."
> "There is only one right way to lead."
> "All leaders are charismatic extroverts."
> "Leaders must never follow."

And so on and so on.

Here's what I've learned, experienced and observed during my 14 years in the NBA that gives me the confidence to tell you that NONE of these statements are true.

**Leadership is like a seed that lies dormant in every one of us.**

In order to germinate, seeds require that certain conditions to be met. You can drop 10 tons of wildflower seeds in the Arctic Circle, but a single flower will not grow. If you take a rosebush and plunk it into the Sahara, the shrub will die. But if you take a seed and then sow it into the Sahara, the seed won't die – it simply won't germinate. That seed will retain its potential for life and growth. If you carry that same kernel to a rainy corner of England and place it in the soil, it will sprout and grow because the conditions support its growth. Leadership is no different.

## The seeds of leadership lie dormant inside each and every one of us.

I'm not referring to plain old, average leadership. I mean great leadership, such as the kind we think of when we hear names like Martin Luther King Jr., Abraham Lincoln, and Gandhi. The potential to become these typles of leader lies inside each of us waiting for the conditions to be met that will allow it to grow. Leadership will automatically develop when these conditions are met.

## The first qualification for leadership is that you succeed at reaching your own goals.

*Only* then can you truly know how to reach down and help someone else to do the same. You can get an MBA from Harvard in Leadership Principles. You can go to leadership conferences and seminars. You can even get a job in a leadership position, but you are not a leader until you have achieved *the goal that completes your life*. I don't mean the goal that you kind-of, sort-of wanted to achieve. It's the goal that *burned inside of you like a fire*. The dream that kept you up at night. The vision that made everything else pale by comparison.

## Leaders accept final responsibility for outcomes.

There is a Chinese parable about an old monk. This old monk was the spiritual leader of a small village. One day, a teenage girl got pregnant. She was confronted by her angry parents who demanded to know who the father was. The girl was scared and told her parents that the old monk was the baby's father. Angry, the parents went to the old monk and told them that they knew he was the father of their daughter's child. The old monk simply nodded his head and all he said was, "Is that so." The villagers stopped attending the monk's services. And, when the baby was born, the girl's parents took the child to the monk saying, "This is your responsibility. You must provide for the child." The monk took the child and said only, "Is that so."

For a year, the monk cared for the child. Finally, the girl admitted to her parents that the monk was not the father of the child. The real father was one of the hired hands at a neighbor's farm. Her parents immediately went to the monk and took the child back, apologizing for the trouble. The monk, upon hearing the news, simply handed the child back and said, "Is that so?"

Now, I don't know about you, but I'm no Zen monk. I'd be pretty upset if a girl slandered me like that; but I've got to admit, this Zen monk is an amazing leader. Why? Because he exemplifies one of the most important traits that a leader possesses: the ability to, without ego, defense or justification, accept final responsibility.

You don't have to be the most extroverted or charismatic person in the world to accept final responsibility. In fact, being charismatic or extroverted has absolutely nothing to do with it. Some of the most effective leaders in the world have been reserved." Think aboutNelson Mandela and Mahatma Gandhi, individuals whoeach possessed quiet leadership, strength of character, discipline, responsibility.Remember, it's not your personality traits that matter as a leader. It's your standards, your convictions, and your example that matter most.

As another example, my mentors like Ambassador Andrew Young or Bishop Eddie L. Long never lift a finger to pawn off responsibility onto another person. Even if the responsibility wasn't theirs, they accept the information and work to make the situation better. They do all this with no gossiping, no griping and no defending their ego.

Like the monk in our story, their vision is so much greater than any personal ego. They are able to set aside the natural knee-jerk reaction to defend themselves and they simply get on with moving toward the goal.

All of the leaders we've discussed thus far lead with a quiet authority that stems from strong vision, unshakeable personal integrity and the ability to accept responsibility with grace and forward motion.

Now, as a coach, the vision is to win games. Coach John Wooden is famous for his attention to detail. But what is less publicized is his unyielding acceptance of responsibility. He doesn't insist that each player on his team be taught to tie his shoelaces in the same way because he wants it to look pretty. Players have been injured on the court from laces that have come undone at just the wrong moment. Now, anyone else would have ignored this seemingly insignificant detail – or would have made it the player's responsibility. Not Coach Wooden.

Even though, technically, the injuries resulting from players' untied laces were not the responsibility of the coach, Wooden took the feedback from the situation and worked immediately to make it better. He did it because how you do anything is how you do everything. Even though it seems like such a tiny example of responsibility, this is indicative of how Coach Wooden ran his team … and his life.

It's the same with you. How you do the little things is indicative of how you deal with responsibility as a leader. This isn't to suggest that you should walk around in deep guilt and misery, adopting some "poor-me" attitude toward the world. Of course, there are things that are out of your control. But, as a team player, you can keep a tighter circle around the things that you do take responsibility for.

For instance, my coach once rocked my world and told me that even if I missed every shot, it was *my* job to take the open shots. It was *his* job to play me or not. My circle of responsibility was much smaller than his. This is vitally important for the development of true leadership.

Oftentimes in the NBA, or in any organization, a star performer will be immediately moved into a position of leadership based on talent – not on his or her ability to lead. The reasoning is that the team needs the star to be a leader and the higher-ups want him to learn how to be a leader as quickly as possible. This is the worst thing to do – for the star, for the other players, for the coach and for the team.

In order to lead, you must know how to obey – or how to follow. That seems backwards, doesn't it? But, it's a universal truth. What is interesting is that it isn't only about knowing how to obey authority figures. You must learn to trust the authorities to maintain their larger circles of responsibility. Plus, you must learn how to maximize your effectiveness within your smaller circles. This doesn't happen overnight.

Think of a rubber band. If you take a rubber band and stretch it out further than it is capable of stretching, it will break. And depending upon how strong the rubber band is, it could do some damage to things in the vicinity when it does break. But, if you take the *same* rubber band and slowly stretch it over time, it will be able to stretch much further and encompass more. The same applies to your circles of responsibility – they don't, and can't, grow overnight.

You have to learn to become accountable to yourself and to take on more and more responsibility. As your tolerance for accepting responsibility – and the accompanying risks and consequences – increases, you are given more responsibility to learn to handle. Until you are able to look at a simple twisted ankle on the court like Coach Wooden, and (instead of immediately saying it is not your responsibility) you learn to naturally and immediately embrace the issues and discover new ways to make the team more able to achieve the vision.

Philosopher and author, John C. Maxwell says, "A leader can give up anything – except final responsibility." Perhaps another way of looking at it is to imagine the people you have known that seem to have made a career out of avoiding responsibility. I can tell you with 100% certainty that these people are missing out – even when it seems like they're not. Not missing out in the sense that would try to diminish their value as human beings, but missing out in the sense that they lose out on opportunity after opportunity. They miss out because they aren't prepared.

They lose self-respect and dignity on a daily basis. They live in a state of perpetual victimization. These are the last people that you would choose to lead a team. Sometimes what happens is that a very charismatic person is also a master at evading responsibility. We've seen this in certain religious or political leaders. Being an effective, long-term leader isn't about charisma, extroversion, or "being born" that way. It simply boils down to accepting responsibility. That and realizing that there's not one right way to lead. I've seen all kinds of leaders in my life and career. . For example, I'll compare two great leaders and coaches I've had the privilege of working with and being led by in my career (through college and the NBA).

They are extremely different and unique in their leadership styles, yet both very effective and successful. I can look over my career and life and see how the leadership styles of both these men helped form the leader I've become today:

| Coach Larry Brown | Coach Jud Heathcote |
| --- | --- |
| Points out areas where you excel to help you stay motivated to perform well. | Points out areas you need to improve to help motivate you to do better. |
| Puts a high emphasis on teaching and consistency | Puts a high emphasis on preparation and details |
| Has a great understanding of how to help you respect the game while keeping a humble spirit and strong character – both in basketball and life | Has a great understanding for when those he leads need assurance; Always finds a way to make things better; Helps develop independent nature in those he leads |

Now shut off the doubts and myths about leadership floating around in your head. Shut them off so you can grow into yourself and into the leadership role in your life, whether it is as a father or mother, a sales associate, or a team player. The role doesn't matter. What does matter is that you accept responsibility and build from there. Simply "run the point." That's exactly what I did, and I'm thankful for it.

# Chapter 3:

# Leaders are More Than Managers

*"The only place that success is before work is in the dictionary."*

**~ Unknown**

During my years of observing, learning and leading, I've come to understand something important: being a good manager and being a good leader are not the same. So what makes a great leader?

**Leaders have the unique ability to create action
in others where there was no action.**

It isn't enough to be able to give orders or teach a concept. Leadership begins when one person takes that critical step forward toward a goal because you encouraged them.

It is impossible to explain exactly what it takes to inspire action in others. What might motivate one person to take action might make another person freeze. For this reason, leaders must be very sensitive to those they lead. They must be able to accurately read others in order to know what inspires and motivates them to take those critical first steps forward.

**Leaders understand the difference between Control and Trust**

Leadership is not based on the ability to <u>control</u> a situation. It is based on the ability to create <u>trust</u>. Leaders create a vision that players can trust and buy into. Too often, the ability to lead is mistaken for the ability to control people, and controlling people never works over the long haul. Think of how many times you have heard people carelessly say the following:

"He made me do this."
"She made me do that."
"I had no choice in the matter."

People who make statements like these believe that others have the ability to control them. If you look closely, you will see that this is never true. Some choices are harder to make than others, and some have steeper consequences. However, we can *always* make a choice.

Many of us, I'm sure, have heard the stories of POWs and victims of torture who have been through the most ghastly and soul numbing experiences imaginable. We can all learn from these people. If they can maintain free will in situations beyond my ability to imagine, then I can avoid falling into a victim mentality in my own life.

**If you notice, great leaders do not subscribe to a victim mentality.**

Great leaders – the ones who inspire trust in their people —have the attitude that everything in their life happens for them, not to them. You can't trust someone who is constantly at the mercy of everyone and everything in their environment. You want to put your faith in those people who are strong enough to be the tree that provides shelter to others, the people who are strong enough to realize and understand and accept that in life that while bad things may happen, one does not have to assume a victim mentality.

One of the most powerful things you can do as a leaders to eliminate the victim mentality from your consciousness. Look back and find a time during your life when you felt victimized. Even if you can't find the point when you had a choice, find the time *after* the event where you had the choice to wallow in the aftermath of it or get on with your life.

Now, please don't misunderstand me here. I don't mean to suggest that there isn't an appropriate time for grief and reacting to traumatic events. What I am talking about here is eliminating the lingering excuses for not getting on with your life. Remember, you can fool the whole world with trumped up defenses and justifications, but you can't fool yourself. You know when you are having a pity party and when you are genuinely experiencing grief.

**To lead effectively, a leader must be willing to take a "fearless moral inventory," to borrow a phrase from Alcoholics Anonymous.**

You must be willing to look at yourself and see the traits that make you great without false modesty AND see the most terrible parts of yourself without defense or justification. The only people who can create trust in the people they lead are the people who have taken a fearless look at the places where they would like to hide behind a victim mentality.

Here's one of my favorite examples of this. This is a true story from a friend of a friend:

> "It was late one night, and I was driving home from a dinner party. I was alone in my car, driving the speed limit when, out of nowhere, a semi truck ran a red light and crashed into my car. My car spun off the road and flipped over in a ditch where I was trapped until the paramedics arrived.
>
> My right arm was broken in three places. The irresponsibility of that truck driver ended my college

football career. I had a good shot at playing pro ball. But all I have to show for the years of hard work and sacrifice is a bum arm and a couple of trophies."

That is one version of the story. Here's the other version when he was asked to look at the same incident without the filter of self-defense, justification and victimization.

"I had been out at a dinner party that night. It was raining and it was late, about 2 a.m. I'd had a couple of beers with dinner, and I was exhausted from mid-terms. I decided to drive home even though my buddy offered to let me sleep on the couch.

I was coming around the corner. Technically, I was going the speed limit, but it was raining and late, and I wasn't at my best, so I didn't have time to stop when the traffic light changed to yellow. It was still my right of way, so I decided to gun it through the intersection. My front wheels were over the line when the light turned red, so I wasn't faulted in the collision. But, should I have slowed down and stopped on the yellow? Yes."

How many people do you know who live in the first story, stubbornly blaming their failures and disappointments on other people and bad luck? How far does this attitude get them in their lives? Would you choose to put your future success, your career, your hopes and dreams in *their* hands? Of course not, because they can't even make the best out of *their* situations. How would they ever be able to help any one else?

The guy in that story is an amazing guy. Not everyone is willing to take such an honest look at his or her story; but I'll tell you this: Its people like him that I turn to for advice, help and leadership.

**Leaders earn the right to lead.**

The ability to create trust and confidence in the minds and hearts of the people you lead starts with you. You must be able to trust yourself. You can't think that you are at the mercy of an unfair world. People that are highly effective and self-actualized are always the ones that feel autonomous and in charge of their lives and well being.

While in college when I struggled with my free throws, I came to trust my coach (Jud Heathcote) enough to start taking shots. I lacked trust in myself, which he inspired me to feel. He bridged the gap by using the trust that he had built up with me to get me to trust in his decisions. It was his decision to play me, even though I shot 15-for-56 (or 26.8 percent) from the free throw line that season. He expected me to do well, to take the shots. I had to temporarily suspend my own lack of confidence in my abilities and trust in his.

I eventually started to make the shots. I became a better player. Eventually, I was able to regain trust in myself. That never would have happened without the intervention of a great leader. It is essential to have someone on your team that is an excellent manager, but the ability to control details and multitask is not what will create a winning team. The ability to create a vision and create trust around it is the one thing that *will* create change.

Trust implies instinctive, unquestioning belief and reliance upon something. To have confidence in a leader implies that the trust is evident because of definite evidence or past experience. Trust and confidence lead to the ability to create the expectation of success – the vision.

How do great leaders create trust in their players or team members? They walk their talk. They have impeccable integrity. They are not afraid to apologize, make amends, or reconsider their actions or behavior. They do not indulge in special treatment, and they do not look to their players, peers or family for validation of their self-worth. They simply walk their talk. To be trusted, they make themselves trustworthy.

Part of being a leader in today's world is looking at the team members as whole people – not just as athletes, or salespeople, or employees or fellow PTA members. Show your team that you care about them as people first and foremost. Then care about them as players, employees or co-workers second. You are guaranteed to earn their trust if you do. This approach to leadership boosts sales, increases efficiencies and wins more games than ever before. It just makes sense that when people are functioning at their best; they will be able to *do more* and *do better* for their team. And they want to because they trust that their leaders have their best interests at heart.

But today's leaders are finding themselves in the role of mentor and point guard. When people start looking to the leader as a mentor, it can be all too easy for that leader to become arrogant and self-righteous. That process takes a little while, though. First, the ego is slightly inflated, and the person starts to believe that he or she does have all the answers. Then there is more validation from the team members when they look to the leader for guidance. That is the reason that so many leaders start off as humble, self-effacing servants and end up becoming narcissistic. As a leader, it is critical to keep your ego in check. Not doing so will make it difficult to motivate your team members and communicate effectively because it becomes all about the leader. He or she is no longe a 'servant leader' who communicates a vision and can bring a team together. .

I call this Edging God Out, or EGO. I have used this phrase often in my life to remind me that, when I think that I have all the answers or that I am irreplaceable, I am only a *servant* of God. Whatever name you call Him, when you accept HIS leadership of yourself and others, you become a servant to His vision and to His teammates. Some people who have never served in a leadership position assume that being a leader is glamorous and exciting. But that isn't what makes a leader great. The philosopher Seneca said, "It is impossible to imagine anything which better becomes a ruler than *mercy.*" Mercy – showing compassion and caring towards a person in one's power. This is what leaders who inspire trust in others do effortlessly.

## Leaders Have a Powerful Personal Vision

There have been numerous books written on this important topic. Long before I understood the need to have a goal and a vision, I could see myself as a professional athlete. Your vision has to be believable, and most importantly, by you. It doesn't matter what the world believes is possible for you. What matters is what *you* believe is possible for you.

I believed that I could be a professional athlete, and I was surrounded by people who believed in me when I didn't. When you have a vision for yourself, it should push you to your absolute limits. I was a talented athlete from a small mid-western city with a brother who made it to the NFL, so I had proof that it could happen. Becoming a professional athlete wasn't something that only happened to other people. Of course, I had doubts along the way. In college, I had so many doubts that I actually had a back-up plan. I was going to work at Ford Motor Company (or to any one of the three auto companies in Michigan) to put myself through graduate school. Or I'd planned to become a graduate assistant at Michigan State University under Coach Izzo who was taking over for Coach Heathcote that next season. I'd thought things through. At the same time, I knew the NBA was possible.

In addition to having a vision, you have to execute, and execution is everything. *Think and Grow Rich* is a catchy book title, but it has been misleading for a lot of people. Sure, you have to have a vision, but you have to put in the legwork to make that vision a reality, too. Taking action toward your dreams can be scary for a lot of people – especially if you let doubt and insecurity sabotage your vision.

The best antidote is self-confidence. I don't mean a cocky or arrogant self-confidence. I mean being confident in your ability to start a task and see it through. If you don't feel that you can finish a task, then you have no incentive to begin.

However, if you have a personal vison and the ability to persevere, make good decisions and practice a solid work ethic, you will be ready to pursue your goals.

## Losing Your Agenda

It can be easy to get an inflated ego when asked to step up and take on a leadership role. A leader must have a strong vision and the conviction to communicate that vision and get the team on-board with that vision. (I will share more with you later on how to share your vison with your team and why this is so crucial). For now, I simply want to stress the importance of being firm in your commitment to your vision. Without an unwavering confidence in your vision, it will be nearly impossible to communicate it to your team and have them support it as well. A leader may have to make modifications to his or her strategy at times, but their vision must be rock solid if he expects others to not only support the vison, but work hard to execute it.

## Just Belief Isn't Enough

Vision is belief with blinders on. You must have a vision of yourself achieving your goals, and be so firm and steadfast in your commitment to your vision that nothing can make you deviate from it. Put blinders on your belief, and focus on the vision that you have inside your heart. This will allow you to keep distractions out and stay inwardly focused. All distractions are equal. There are no minor distractions. You must be single-minded in the pursuit of your goal. We all make mistakes and fall off the path at times, but the trick is to not to use those small deviations as excuses to continue down the wrong road. Get back on track and put the blinders back on, because belief is not enough. Even vision alone is not enough.

## You have to *expect* success.

You have to know and expect that success is possible. There's no guarantee that it *will* happen. For example, my not making an NBA roster wouldn't necessarilymean that I wasn't good enough or that I failed. What it would mean is that there are fifteen guys ahead of me. When you are going into a make-it-or-break-it game, it isn't enough to believe that you are going to win. The magic happens when the team comes together and *expects* to win. This is vision in action.

A lot of people avoid expectations because they are afraid they will be disappointed - even devastated - if the expectations aren't met. However, I encourage you to look at this in a different light. If you have self confidence and trust your ability to achieve your goals and keep your promises, then you know that there is no failure – only feedback.

If I go out onto the court and I expect to win but we lose, I am not crushed by the experience. Nor is my team. We simply look at our performance, learn from our mistakes, improve on our strengths and, without compromising our mental fortitude, go out there the next night and expect to win again. Having a strong vision allows you to do this, no matter how many times you lose.

If you have a combination of the right mindset, a powerful work ethic and the expectation of success, the only way that you can fail is by giving up too soon. Eventually you will succeed. It is just a matter of time.

**But beware! One thing that we do to sabotage our success is refusing to *commit to* our vision.**

Whether your vision is to become a ball player in the NBA, to lead your company's sales records, or to get your master's degree, when that vision lands in your head, take a snapshot of it just as it is. Write it down. Immediately. Don't worry if it is the *right* vision or if it is a *possible* vision or if other people will like the vision. Press freeze-frame and examine it. If you have trouble focusing on it, then try pretending that it is the vision of someone you love. If this was your wife's vision or your best friend's vision, wouldn't you let it have a little more space to exist before you shut it down?

What we tend to do is move around between visions – or we keep reworking a vision until it is "perfect." The truth is your vision was perfect the moment it popped into your mind. Constantly picking at the vision is just another way to avoid doing the work that needs to be done to achieve it. We can get so caught up in analysis that it turns into a kind of paralysis. We analyze the vision from every angle: "Well, I could get a master's in business, but maybe a master's in economics would be better. And what school will I go to? How will I pay for it?"

This type of analysis leads to fear, doubt and insecurity. Before you know it, you inner voice is saying: "I can't even pay my bills now, so how can I expect to go to school, work and pay tuition?" And you become paralyzed.

My vison was to play in the NBA. It was a simple, complete and perfect vision. If I had overworked my vision, it would have looked more like this: "I want to play in the NBA, but I'm afraid that I'm not talented enough" or, "My dream is to play in the NBA, but I'm also good at football." When this happens, the power of your vision becomes diluted as you find more and more bits of 'proof' to delay taking action.

The most powerful visons are the simple ones. However you may find yourself running into a few stumbling blocks as you work to define a vision for yourself. For example, some leaders think they have a vision but barely think about it. If you find yourself *under* thinking your vision, this might indicate that it really isn't the best vision for you. Or perhaps you find yourself trying to accept someone else's vision for you and carve yourself into *their* mold. (Children often do this, especially with visions their parents' may unwittingly encourage them to pursue – and these are often visions they as parents did not!)

The best way to make sure you have chosen the right vision for yourself is to simply sit with your vision for while. Give it days, weeks, or even months to become a part of you. Don't try to turn your life upside down to follow the vision if it doesn't feel right to you. If it does feel right, then charge right ahead. The truth is that you can't really deny the call to action your vision will inspire in you if it is the right one.

If you have kept with me up until this point, it is time that you hear the challenges of leadership. It is a hard job that requires you to abandon your personal agenda for the good of your team. You carry the stress of making the decisions, often split-second choices that determine the results for the team and, often, the careers of the team members.

When I was having free-throw trouble, my coaches (Heathcote and Izzo) had faith and belief in me that impacted me and my future. They held the futures of all of the players in their hands. What a huge responsibility! At the time, I only saw their faith and belief in me. I didn't see the great responsibility that they gracefully and humbly managed on a daily basis until now. I wasn't meant to see it. They weren't good leaders – they were *great* leaders, coaches and mentors who consistently showed only encouragement and support.

There is a saying in business that goes, "Talk *up* to your downline and talk *down* to your upline." This means that you only bring the members of your team up with your language and message. You can talk down – get out your frustrations and concerns – with your mentors.

Leadership is, in my experience, a very special and rewarding responsibility that definitely has its moments. But, for the most part, it is, as Winston Churchill put it, "One damn thing after another."

## Thoughts on Leadership by Daniel Gibson, Cleveland Cavaliers

**What are the top three qualities of a good leader?**
A good leader must be strong minded, vocal and trusted.

**What are the top three faults of a bad leader?**
A bad leader is somebody who is does not respond with confidence when he gets caught in a tough situation. A bad leader is untrustworthy. A bad leader is also a bad communicator, someone who can't talk to teammates when things get rough.

**Who are or were the three most important leaders in your life and why?**
My father, Byron Gibson, was very important in my life because, in any situation, he just said what he felt was the right thing for me, even if I didn't want to hear it – even if I didn't ask for advice. My grandmother, Janice Hardeman, passed away two years ago. Throughout my life, she had been there so much for me. She always had inspirational words for me. Then there's Isiah Thomas. I used to watch him play. He was a leader on the floor. He motivated his teammates. You knew he was going to someday be a coach.

**In your opinion, who were the three top leaders in NBA history and why do you feel that way?**
My first answer would have to be Michael Jordan because of everything he accomplished. I've never had a chance to be around him, but I've heard stories, like how he motivated those guys to compete every night. Now, Magic Johnson was different than Mike. He led by his smile. In tough situations, he made things seem like they were still going to be alright. Finally, I'd have to say Phil Jackson. By any means necessary, he figures out a way to get through to his players – the Zen Buddha. I've heard about of a lot of different situations in which he found a way to reach his players, a way to relate.

**In your opinion, who are the top three leaders in the league today and why do you feel that way?**

My number one pick would be LeBron James. He is a mirror image of Magic. He leads by the way he carries himself, how he carries himself on the floor. He's a big-time motivator off the floor, always gets us going in the right direction. I'd make Kobe Bryant second. He lifts his teammates. He has evolved into one of our best leaders. He went through some things that, over time, that changed his personality. This year he took his team to the finals. They trusted him. Third, I'd choose Chris Paul. I know Chris personally. I've been around him. He doesn't care how certain guys feel or how it might make them feel to if he says something to them. He's tough-minded. If he feels like something is best for the team in a certain moment, he's going to say it. He has that quality.

# Chapter 4:

## Discovering Your Leadership Style

*"If you can tell me who your heroes are,*
*I can tell you how you're going to turn out in life."*

**-Warren Buffett**

In my study of life and leadership during my years in the NBA, I have found that, in order to become a great leader – or a great basketball player, or a great father, or a great business owner – you must immerse yourself in the study of those who are *already* great and who personify what you are trying to attain.

That is why I wanted to share with you, my "Top Ten" mentors, heroes and successful leaders. I respect, study and pray to emulate these people in my day-to-day life. Doing this has made all the difference in my life.

1. Bishop Eddie Long: a visionary, great communicator, innovative, charismatic

2. Ambassador Andrew Young: courageous, personifies sacrifice, full of integrity

3. Pat Croce: passionate, assertive, analytical

4. William Hunter: patient, savvy, excellent communicator

5. Dikembe Mutombo: noble, persistent, engaging

6. Joe Dumars: humble, disciplined, consistent

7. Larry Brown: encouraging, nurturing, empathetic

8. Mayor Shirley Franklin: ambitious, adaptable, decisive

9. Xernona Clayton: kind, engaging, creative

10. Roland Warren: ambitious, motivating, enthusiastic

Each of these men and women have shown me or shared with me, through their everyday deeds and memorable triumphs, some of the secrets to their success. From the patience of Joe Dumars to the passion of Pat Croce to the people skills of Andrew Young and Dikembe Mutombo, these leaders are all worth learning about. In telling their stories, I can reveal some of what I've learned from them.

## Bishop Eddie L. Long

A true visionary and spiritual force of nature, Bishop Long became pastor at New Birth Missionary Baptist Church in 1987 when the congregation numbered only about 300 people. He always saw bigger things. He always believed in his God-inspired message and in God's promises.

Today, through his teachings and preaching on the Trinity Broadcast Network, through his ten books, and through the Sunday sermons he delivers at his arena-sized church in suburban Atlanta, Bishop Long has grown his flock to more than 25,000 members.

After the 2006 passing of Coretta Scott King, the widow of the Rev. Martin Luther King Jr., ten thousand mourners packed into Bishop Long's massive cathedral to say goodbye. That crowd was joined by President George W. Bush, first lady Laura Bush, U.S. Senator Hillary Clinton and former Presidents Bill Clinton, George H.W. Bush and Jimmy Carter. That day, Bishop Long gave the nation a place to grieve.

He remains a man of so much insight and inspiration. The mission of New Birth is to lead the world to worship God through serving, loving, evangelizing and making disciples. His orations are a call to action. Bishop Long is a true evangelist whose moving delivery and potent Gospel messages carry a practical application in today's world.

Still, he's willing to throw on his work clothes and dig into modern problems, including leading young people to better days. In 2004, Bishop Long put together a mentorship program called the LongFellows Summer Academy. It provides experiences geared toward the mental, physical and spiritual development of boys between the ages of 13 and 18. Bishop Long raised enough money to pay for scholarships for 63 of the academy's members that year.

He has taught me lessons on brotherhood and sharing. He is a believer in strong teaching and sharing of the deeds of faith toward others. Bishop Long comes to his friends and supporters like a protective big brother who not only gives you security but encourages you to one day stand on your own.

## Dikembe Mutombo

He has come a long way in this world, yet he never left home. There's something to be said for that. One of the things I admire most about Dikembe is that he not only remembers his roots, he has devoted his life to making his native land a healthier and happier place.

He was born in Kinshasa, the capital city of the Democratic Republic of the Congo in central Africa, and is the seventh of ten children. His lean body stretches to a 7-foot-2-inch tower. But unlike American kids with the same stature, he never saw himself earning huge paychecks in the NBA. Dikembe wanted to be a doctor.

In 1987, he arrived at Georgetown University in Washington, D.C. on an academic scholarship. He planned to study medicine, eventually earn his degrees and return to the Congo and practice medicine. But in this country, people see a man of that size and they instantly think one thing: NBA.

During Dikembe's second year at Georgetown, head basketball coach John Thompson asked him to try out for the powerhouse Hoyas hoops team. With just a rough grasp of English and an even rougher handle on the game, Dikembe managed to earn a spot on the elite squad. He never abandoned his books – working toward dual degrees in linguistics and diplomacy – yet he also immersed himself in basketball and became a star, transforming himself into an NCAA scoring threat and master shot-blocker. As far as I'm concerned, he is the poster boy for squeezing the most out of your time: learning five languages and leading Georgetown to three NCAA tournament appearances.

Of course, with his deep talent, the NBA soon called – and the money soon flowed. Dikembe was drafted by the Denver Nuggets in 1991, and helped turn that franchise from doormat to winner. Next it was on to Atlanta, Philadelphia, New Jersey, New York and Houston, usually helping each club thrive. During what has become a distinguished, seventeen-season career, Dikembe has earned NBA Defensive Player of the Year honors four times and banked more than $100 million in salary. It is off the court where Dikembe has truly done wonders, though – just as he had planned to do years ago.

He began spending his off seasons traveling throughout Africa, performing at free basketball clinics for two thousand kids a day, visiting Somali refugee camps in Northern Kenya, and touring Cape Town and Johannesburg with NBA Commissioner David Stern and former Georgetown players Patrick Ewing and Alonzo Mourning. And, of course, he came back to Kinshasa and spread some good medicine. He tapped his NBA riches to start the Dikembe Mutombo Foundation, which aims to eradicate the childhood diseases that still threaten the lives of children in the Congo.

In the league, Dikembe is famous for swatting shots, waving his index finger and shouting, "No one flies in the House of Mutombo!" In life, we all should pay a visit to the House of Mutombo. This is a man who understands what is important and how to get the important things done.

He is a world leader who shows everyone the value of blending hard work and a global vision. To me, he stands for strong education, longevity and consistency.

## Larry Brown

During a sparkling career built on thousands of victories, Coach Brown may have revealed the best part of his character in losing. True leaders, like this man, know that to make it up the mountain, sometimes you have to trudge through the trenches.

A Brooklyn native, he played college ball at North Carolina and then logged five pro seasons – averaging 11.2 points per game – in the old American Basketball Association. He won an ABA title with the Oakland Oaks in 1969, and set an ABA record by dishing twenty-three assists in one game for Denver in 1972. With his knack for connecting with people and for teaching and motivating, he was destined to be the man calling the shots. He is a natural coach.

That journey has taken him through more than twenty NBA seasons – and seven years at the college ranks – all the way to a spot in the Naismith Memorial Basketball Hall of Fame.

He is a man who knows how to build a résumé. Coach Brown has pushed his NBA teams to eight seasons of fifty wins or more, seven divisional titles, three conference championships (Philadelphia in 2001 and Detroit in 2004 and 2005) and one World Championship with the Pistons in 2004. As a college coach, he won the national title at the University of Kansas in 1988. In the Olympics, he led American squads (as the head coach or assistant coach) to the bronze medal in 2004, at Athens and the gold in 2000, at Sydney. As a player, he also earned an Olympic gold medal at the 1964, Tokyo Games. In fact, he is the only American man to play *and* coach basketball at the Olympics.

But one of Coach Brown's most impressive moments came during and after a disastrous year as the leader of the New York Knicks. He arrived in the Big Apple in 2005 with big expectations. He left after just one season. His New York team, snarled by inner turmoil, notched just twenty-three wins in eighty-two games.

How did he react to all that losing in America's media capital? He stood up and stayed accountable. He blamed himself. He didn't duck from questions or criticism. He found lessons in the bad times. And then he moved forward. "I was a bad coach. I did a bad job. I learned from that," Coach Brown has said.

He stayed off the NBA benches for two years, viewing the game carefully from afar, watching how other men coached, dissecting how the style of the game was changing to favor guard play, figuring out – all over again – just what it takes to win in modern basketball. Then, in 2008, he landed another job as head coach of the Charlotte Bobcats.

Coach Brown has an iron-strong belief in doing things the right way, all the time. He is a master communicator who teaches that no one member is greater than the whole, and that preparation and work ethic are the great equalizers.

## Joe Dumars

Never flashy and always in charge, Joe has forged a potent career on the strength of his integrity and the power of conviction. He has always known who he is and has always believed in what he was doing. I think that comes from his parents.

Born in the small Louisiana town of Natchitoches, Joe was raised by a truck driving dad, "Big Joe," and a custodian mom, Ophelia. Not surprisingly, their rise-at-dawn, labor-all-day mentality was forged into Joe's DNA.

As a member of the rough-and-tumble Detroit Pistons teams of the late 1980s and '90s – the "Bad Boys," they were called – Joe shared the backcourt with the supremely talented Isiah Thomas. While Isiah and his bright smile soaked up most of the limelight, Joe's timely scoring landed him on six NBA All-Star teams while his sweat at the other end of the court put him on four all-NBA defensive teams. In other words: he was always working. At the same time, he earned respect from other players. While his frontcourt teammates built reputations as bulky bruisers, Joe was the first recipient of the NBA's sportsmanship award which today is called the Joe Dumars Trophy.

After retiring from the game, Joe joined the workforce as a business man. He proved he could run a company as deftly as he ran the Detroit offense. He founded and became majority owner, CEO and president of Detroit Technologies, an automotive supply company. In 2006, he sold his interest in the business but stayed in auto parts – well Pistons, anyway. He now serves as Detroit's president of basketball operations. He assembled the roster that won the NBA title in 2004 and threatened to rip it down again when he didn't like the effort his players turned in during the 2008 Eastern Conference Finals against Boston. Following the Pistons' ouster in that series, Joe fired his head coach, Flip Saunders, then put his stars on notice that they might be packing soon, too. A leader can never be afraid to act boldly or instill discipline.

Still a silent leader, Joe has always believed that time is the ultimate vindicator. He has shown me that humility and character count.

## Roland Warren

Before he put his energy and Ivy League smarts behind the crucial cause of fatherhood in America, Roland seemed destined to become a CEO on Wall Street. He still may accomplish that, but right now, he's doing some of America's most critical work.

As a younger man, Roland received his MBA from the prestigious Wharton School at the University of Pennsylvania. He became a financial consultant for Goldman Sachs in Philadelphia, worked as an associate director of development for his undergraduate alma mater, Princeton University, and took management positions at IBM and PepsiCo.

In 2001, two leaders of the National Fatherhood Initiative left that non-profit organization to take jobs with the Bush Administration. The NFI's board of directors immediately elevated Roland from executive vice president to president.

The mission of the initiative, based in Maryland, is to improve the well being of children by increasing the proportion of kids who grow up with involved, responsible and committed fathers. They accomplish this through education and awareness campaigns, research projects, training and business partnerships.

For example, after Oprah Winfrey broadcast a program she called "The Secret Thoughts of Fathers," she invited Roland to the show to speak about the value of fatherhood and the damage children suffer when dads are absent. Later, Roland was asked to moderate a roundtable discussion about husbands and fathers that was published in *O, the Oprah Magazine.* He has even taken on the modern message of Father's Day – how greeting cards that are written and produced for that holiday have generally reduced the role of dads to punch lines about fishing, drinking beer and watching TV. Fathers are portrayed as "dumb, dangerous or disaffected," Roland protested to a newspaper in 2008.

While absentee fatherhood remains a large issue, Roland has said that the dads who *are* involved tend to be more committed and take a more hands-on approach than they typically experienced with their own fathers while growing up. Of course, most importantly, Roland and his wife, Yvette, have two sons of their own.

Roland shares my passion for the inclusion of men – especially fathers – in forging strong families and communities. He is a builder and supporter of men.

### Shirley Franklin

Shirley offers a timeless lesson: seizing what's possible in this world while at the same time never giving in to doubt and never playing it safe.

Even though she had never been elected to a public office, Shirley decided to run for mayor in 2001 in a major U.S. city – a city that had never elected a female and in a region of the country that had never elected an African-American woman to any office. Tall odds? She won in a landslide, becoming the fifty-eighth mayor of Atlanta.

The voters saw that she had put in the necessary work and that she was smart, diligent and ready for the job. Although she is originally from Philadelphia, Mayor Franklin had learned the inner workings and society of Atlanta. Long before grabbing office, she had earned a Bachelors of Arts degree in Sociology from Howard University and, later, a Master of Arts degree in Sociology from the University of Pennsylvania. Sociology, of course, is the study of the intricacies of human society. In other words, she knows people.

In 1978, she took her first steps in public service, working for then Atlanta Mayor Maynard Jackson as the commissioner of cultural affairs. Next, under then Mayor Andrew Young, she became the nation's first woman chief administrative officer, or city manager – a job that left her responsible for all of Atlanta's daily operations. It was like running a $1 billion dollar company with 8,000 employees. Her deft management in that role eventually convinced voters that she was ready to run and represent the entire city.

At city hall, Mayor Franklin hurled herself into the gritty work of bolstering Atlanta's government machinery: boosting its accountability, tightening the efficiency of city operations and building partnerships with private and non-profit entities in the area – the essential, albeit non-glitzy, chores of a successful civic leader.

Her checklist of successes has touched a variety of issues. Mayor Franklin launched one of the most robust ethics reform programs in the nation. She laid the foundation for the current $3.2 billion overhaul of the city's aging water and sewer system. She completed the fifth runway at Hartsfield-Jackson Atlanta International Airport as part of a $6.3 billion airport investment plan. She commissioned city leaders to study homelessness in the city to develop the "Blueprint to End Chronic Homelessness in Atlanta in 10 years." Additionally, she started the New Century Economic Development Plan, outlining an economic vision through 2009 that includes aggressive redevelopment and affordable housing and transportation goals.

A progressive leader, Mayor Franklin has cast a forward-thinking vision that attracts and taps people who are ready to make a change.

## Pat Croce

Blessed with a boundless zest for life and a heart that never stops dreaming, Pat has built a feel-good empire.

At the core of his world lies the physical body: his devotion to building, bolstering and celebrating our natural, physical tools and all the places they can take us. What's the difference between your run-of-the-mill fitness nut and Pat? His passion. I can think of few people who have more fire.

Always a gym rat, Pat played college football at a small school in Pennsylvania before transferring to the University of Pittsburgh to earn a degree in physical therapy and a certification in athlete training. His first hope was to become the Philadelphia Eagles' head physical therapist. The team said no. Pat learned how to wait and keep striving. He worked for a while as physical therapist at a suburban Philadelphia hospital until he finally landed a job in 1980 as the conditioning coach for the Philadelphia Flyers.

His sweat-drenched workouts with the hockey players quickly became legend among other pro athletes in Philly. The Philadelphia 76ers soon asked Pat to apply his methods to their players. As his guru status spread throughout major league sports, he essentially created the concept of personal training – long before there was even a name for the profession.

His entrepreneurial flair next took root. Pat opened a physical therapy/fitness center where he could share his energy and exercise techniques with everyday people. And the clients flocked, eating up his message. In fewer than ten years, that company, Sports Physical Therapists, ballooned from one gym to forty centers in eleven states. In the mid-1990s, Pat pulled off a true sports-business coup, selling his fitness chain and buying a stake in the 76ers. During his five years as president and minority owner, the team rose from a sputtering, last-place club to become a championship contender, as if it were feeding off Pat's electric aura.

Today, Pat continues to be a master motivator and a guy who devours life in big bites. He built the world's first authentic pirate museum – Pirate Soul – in Key West, Florida. And he has injected his unique style into numerous TV appearances, including during

NBA games, Tae Kwon Do matches at the 2004 Summer Olympics in Greece and as the host of a nationally syndicated daily TV show, *Pat Croce: Moving In.*

What I respect about Pat is that he came from average surroundings to make himself into a man of champions. He has a strong belief in the power of the ordinary person to do extraordinary things. He is a true product of hard work, networking, and being at the right place at the right time.

## Xernona Clayton

Let me introduce you to a foot soldier in the civil rights struggle. Xernona has marched, taught, written, investigated, organized and conversed poetically during a long life committed to the upward movement of our people. She's still hard at work today, awarding the key contributions and accomplishments of black men and women in this country.

Xernona and her twin sister, Xenobia, were born in Muskogee, Oklahoma, where their parents administered Indian affairs in the 1930s. That work offered Xernona an early, personal education into the lives of American minorities. It obviously stayed with her.

While attending graduate school at the University of Chicago in the 1950s, Xernona agreed to work for Chicago's Urban League as an undercover agent probing employment discrimination. She was next enticed into two more critical jobs: civil rights negotiation and teaching children. After leaving Chicago, she volunteered for a school drop-out program in Los Angeles. Then, in the early 1960s, she organized fundraisers for the Southern Christian Leadership Conference – the civil rights group led by Dr. Martin Luther King, Jr. Xernona's talent, street-wise background and fervor for the cause quickly caught the attention of Dr. King and his wife, Coretta Scott King. In time, Mrs. King and Xernona became close friends.

She became a media maven, penning pieces for *Atlanta Voice* and becoming the first black woman in the American South to host a regularly scheduled prime-time talk show, *Variations*, in 1968. The program later became *The Xernona Clayton Show* on WAGA-TV in Atlanta. Some of her guests included Harry Belafonte and Lena Horne. Her broadcasting work ultimately brought her to Turner Broadcasting where she produced documentaries, hosted *Open Up* – a public affairs program – and earned the title of assistant corporate vice-president for urban affairs.

Her long stroll through the civil rights era inspired her to write and publish an autobiography called *I've Been Marching All the Time* in 1991. Most recently, Xernona and Turner Broadcasting created the Trumpet Awards to honor exceptional African Americans. Honorees in 2008, included actress Halle Berry and Khalil Johnson, CEO of the Georgia World Congress Center Authority.

Xernona cast her lot among giants from whom she could learn. She has never shied from taking advice from elders. Ultimately, she made it her mission to ensure that those worthy of recognition for their places in the struggle for human equality were lauded and thanked while they were still living.

## Ambassador Andrew Young

A warrior for human justice and a fearless practitioner of faith, Ambassador Young continues to build on his legacy of struggle and triumph.

He was raised in a home of discipline by his mother, a school-teacher, and his father, a dentist who loved boxing. Along the way, though, Ambassador Young learned the quiet value of pacifism and the art of peaceful demonstration. In the rural town of Marion, Alabama, he was appointed to serve as a church pastor. There, he also began to study the lessons of non-violent resistance taught by Mohandas Gandhi. He was inspired to lead voter registration drives among African Americans in Alabama and, during that time, he befriended Dr. Martin Luther King, Jr.

As the civil rights movement gained traction in the 1960s, Ambassador Young took up key positions on the front lines of that social battle, continuing to register black voters in Atlanta and joining demonstrations in Selma, Alabama, and St. Augustine, Florida, and going to jail for his role in those marches. In Birmingham, Alabama, he served as a mediator between white and black communities. In 1964, he was named the executive director of the Southern Christian Leadership Conference, learning at the foot of Dr. King. In fact, he was with him in Memphis when Dr. King was assassinated in 1968.

His penchant for changing America soon took him into traditional politics. In the early 1970s, he won and later retained a seat in Congress. In 1977, President Jimmy Carter appointed him as ambassador to the United Nations. And in 1981, he was elected mayor of Atlanta, a job he held for most of that decade. He elevated the city's stature by parlaying international investment into a stronger civic economy. He also lured the 1988 Democratic National Convention to Atlanta.

These days, Ambassador Young is co-chairman of Good Works International, a global advisory firm that offers business connections and political risk analysis of emerging markets in Africa and the Caribbean. Its clients include companies like Chevron, Coca-Cola, Delta Airlines and General Electric.

I have always admired Ambassador Young for his unashamed, unabashed ability to express his rights to be a human being in this society and for challenging others to accept their own humanity.

## Billy Hunter

Whether battling NBA brass on behalf of an immature rookie – or the Hell's Angels biker gang on behalf of the U.S. government, Billy has never backed down from a fight.

The Camden, N.J., native is mostly known for his work within pro basketball circles. But his best sport might have been football. In the 1960s, he graduated from Syracuse University after serving as captain of the Syracuse football team. He flashed his leadership skills on the field and off, organizing his Syracuse teammates to boycott Southern schools with segregated stadiums.

After a two-year NFL career with Miami and Washington, he earned his law degree from Howard University, earned a master of law degree from Cal Berkeley and then worked as a prosecutor in San Francisco. In 1977, after Jimmy Carter appointed him as a United States Attorney, Billy supervised the prosecution of members of Jim Jones' People's Temple and the Hell's Angels, and he advised the president on the pardon of Patricia Hearst. In the 1980s, he opened his own law practice, specializing in municipal finance, entertainment law and white-collar criminal defense.

His took those new-found advocacy skills to the NBA in 1996, earning the high-profile, high-pressure role of executive director of National Basketball Players Association. He served as chief negotiator during crucial labor negotiations that culminated in the 1999 Collective Bargaining Agreement between the NBA and its players. Under that pact, the players were assured of maintaining their status as the best compensated athletes in team sports. Of course, that contract came with some labor pain, but Billy was credited for helping build the solidarity that carried NBA players through the league lockout that delayed the start of the 1998-1999 season by more than two months.

Billy cares for and protects the interests of those people who are not yet mature or developed. He believes deeply in the power of advocacy and, as he has shown, he never surrenders.

## The Common Thread

I'd like to take a few pages to share with you a little of my personal journey and how I developed my own personal leadership style. Why right here and right now, you might ask?

Each of these amazing individuals influenced my leadership style greatly. There are many common themes they all share, and I want to share a few of them with you so that you can understand just how they still continue to influence my life. It is this thread that keeps me connected to them, and influences my leadership style to this day.

I bet if you take a step back, you could do the same thing. Find the leaders and the mentors who did the same for you. That's an important step for you to take in your own leadership journey. Doing so will help you understand your strengths, but will also serve as a standard of leadership greatness you can continue to aspire to. Leaders are always learning. Look at who brought you to where you are today so that you can carry on what they deposited in you. This is a great way to find our how your leadership style was developed. Who better to continue to learn from than those who initially modelled excellent leadership standards **for you in the first place?**

Here are two of the most important lessons I learned, and continue to learn, from those who have shaped me as a leader:

## Learn to control your inner critic.

We all have an inner critic that will take every opportunity to bring us down. If you listen to that critic, you will never take the risks, seize the opportunities and make the choices necessary to reach your dreams. Knowing that you did the best you could do *at that time* is the best antidote to that inner critic that I have ever found. It allows me to keep moving forward in a positive direction rather than spending my time trying to change the past.

You are never going to get ahead if you don't get off your own back and you will never be a great leader if you don't understand that people are always doing the best they can. Your job as a leader will be to encourage them to do better by getting the skills and experience necessary to affect their lives in the most positive way while helping them to move away from wallowing in self-criticism that isn't helping them get better.

The way you learn to do that for other people is to first do it for yourself. Get off the "beat-myself-up" train, and start taking proactive, positive action toward reaching your goals. Big things are made up of little things, and how you do anything is how you do everything. We will talk more about this, but if there is anything I learned from my mentors about reaching your dreams, it is this: *There are no little things. Everything you do moves you toward your dreams or away from them. There is no neutral.*

So silence your inner critic by letting go of any shame or unnecessary anger you may still be holding onto about things that did not go so well in your past. Holding onto to these past failures will stop you dead in your tracks, and keep you from moving forward as a leader.

**Every big goal is nothing but a thousand tiny steps along the way to attaining your dream.**

Another critical lesson I have learned from my mentors is the importance of focusing on the small step right in front of you NOW. For each step in your journey, focus on that one and master it, make it a habit and do it with everything you've got inside of you to give. As you successfully master other important tasks on your way to achieving your goals, you will soon find yourself achieving more than you thought possible and on your way to living your dream.

John Wooden, the legendary and brilliant UCLA basketball coach, believed in this principle so strongly that he taught his players how to tie their shoes when they got to his team. The idea behind this is that even so small a detail as tying shoes could impact the team's ability to achieve their goals. If all the shoes are correctly laced and tied, there is a much smaller risk that one will come untied resulting in a distraction or injury to the player.

Coach Wooden was one of the best builders of winning teams the world has seen – and one of the most beloved and admired leaders in the game. Everyone could learn how to approach life and leadership from this man. There are no little things. Every big thing is just a thousand little things put together. Let me give you a real-life example:

Coming out of junior high as the starting, leading scorer on our basketball team, I was all set for my big-time high school career. I strutted onto the court that first day of practice feeling pretty good about myself. You can imagine how I felt when I found out that I didn't make the starting team! This would be a recurring theme throughout my career, but I didn't know that then. All I knew was that my 15-year-old self was devastated. I had a choice to make: quit or stick it out. The choice that I made when I was 15 years old would impact the rest of my life.

We all make choices like this everyday. This is part of the whole "there-are-no-little-things" idea we were just talking about. Everything that went into making me who I was up until that point came into play at that moment. My father's example, my mother's love, and my coaches' belief in me as a player. All of that went into the most important career decision that I would ever make. Would I quit? Would I accept being second string? Would I accept being a player who was good, but not good enough to start?

If I had accepted that for a moment I wouldn't have made it to the NBA. At 15, I gritted my teeth and decided that if I didn't reach my ultimate goal of becoming a starter, it wouldn't be because I hadn't done every last thing in my power to make the team. So, I worked harder. I didn't settle for being second string. I was determined to make myself a better player so that the coach would *have* to play me. I worked harder that pre-season than I had ever worked before. I didn't know if I was even going to get a chance to play first string, but I knew that I was going to be ready. As it happened, the senior on the starting team got into trouble just before the season started. He wasn't eligible to play the first game. And I was ready. Coach put me into the starting line-up and I was ready to start. I went on to become the top scorer all through high school. I received all-state honors each year and attracted the attention of college scouts. I received invitations to basketball summer camps where talent scouts would be.

I got a basketball scholarship to Michigan State because of that afternoon in the locker room when I looked at the starting lineup and didn't see my name. I didn't know it at the time, but it was that moment – that moment when I *didn't* quit – that gave me a shot at a career in professional basketball. But that wasn't the only one. There were a few other defining moments that would rock my world. They were the conditions that made the leadership seed inside of me sprout. Those moments would take me from a player with potential to a rock-solid player, a clutch player, a player who would become the captain of teams.

I tell you this for a few reasons. First of all, I am not the most talented player to play in the NBA. There are hundreds of players that are more talented than me that *should be* playing in the NBA but who aren't. But it wasn't talent that got me into the NBA. It was my determination and persistence. My willingness to be coachable and to do whatever was within my power to do. It was all those "little things." *Anyone* can do the same thing – in any venture, in any business, in any environment – to reach their dreams.

Danny DeVito is a movie star. He is 5'4" inches tall and isn't anyone's idea of a really good-looking, leading-role guy. He had everything going against him. But he never quit. He was always working on himself, on his skills, on being the best actor he could be. And he has given us some amazing movies.

Oprah Winfrey also had a rough start. We've all heard her story of determination and overcoming obstacles.

None of these people were given a magical ride to success. And none of them were people that the world would have bet on to become successful. Yet, the one thing they never lacked was determination and hard, consistent work. Anyone can get what he or she wants. *Anyone.* You just first have to discover *and believe* that for yourself. You can have and be what you want. Start with the small steps, and keep moving forward, one step at a time. Maybe it will take years of blood, sweat, tears, setbacks and victories before you have achieved what you set out to accomplish. It may take you years to even believe that you can have the life you dream of, or maybe you will believe it today.

Either way, once you believe in your own abilities, you'll then start believing in the abilities of everyone else you meet. In that moment, your leader's heart will naturally push you to share that belief with everyone you meet. That is leadership — true, genuine, magnetic leadership. Most people will walk through fire for you when you have the unshakeable certainty that they can achieve their dreams – and that you'll help them get there.

That moment in the locker room when I realized I was on the second-string list – *that* was my first defining moment. But I chose to keep working. To keep going. To focus on improving the "little things." And you see how it paid off.

Here's the great news. You can choose this path for yourself at any time. If you have given up on your dreams, thought they were unrealistic, impossible or out of reach at any time in your life, *now* is the time that you can take them back. My job is to be prepared to play. *When* I play or *how much* I play, or whether or not I start on the team is out of my control.

But being prepared and ready to play at the highest level I am capable of and being a leader, encourager and mentor to my teammates – that is my business and in my control. It is all I can do … and it has been enough. The same applies to you.

My next defining moments would take a cocky kid and turn him into a man capable of leadership. Those moments came in college. But you'll have to wait a bit to read about that!

## Thoughts on Leadership by Larry Brown, Head Coach of the Charlotte Bobcats

**What are the top three qualities of a good leader?**
The guy has to be real. I have seen a lot of guys that tell people what to do, but they don't necessarily step up to the plate and do the things they want others to do. I think it's important to be real and be a stand-up kind of guy if you expect other people to do what you want. You've got to be a high-character guy. It's much easier to follow somebody you know is a decent guy, who you know that you admire as a person. Also, you can't be afraid to take coaching. When I was looking at my teams, the teams that have been most successful were the ones that accepted coaching.

**What are the top three faults of a bad leader?**
Bad leaders can't accept criticism. If you can't accept coaching, that's a huge problem. Not consistently trying to do the right thing in life is also a sign. If you expect people to follow you, you've got to set an example and do what's right. Everybody knows we don't do what's right all the time, but you have to try to do the right thing. Then there's inconsistency. Guys that aren't good leaders aren't consistent. If you change the things you demand and allow certain things to slide – the things that are important to you – you can't be a good leader.

**Who are or were the three most important leaders in your life and why?**
My high school coach Bobby Gersten was very important to me. He taught me a lot that I carry with me still today. I also had two of the greatest college coaches in Frank McGuire and Dean Smith. I also played for other people who were unbelievable: Hank Iba, Pete Newell, Alex Hannum and John McLendon. Lastly, my dad died when I was really young and Joe Glass became my representative, but he was more like family. He was probably the most decent man I've ever

been around. And my mom was a single parent who raised me and sacrificed everything for me and my brother.

**In your opinion, who were the three top leaders in the history of the game and why do you feel that way?**
I admire Dean Smith. He was a great leader. For instance, his players were known for acknowledging a pass from a teammate after they scored a basket. He helped them understand that it takes a team to become the best. I also admire what Red Auerbach has done as a coach and administrator. I look up to Coach John McLendon for how he conquered the adversity he faced. He's made great contributions – not only to integrating basketball, but to the game itself. Michael Jordan was a great, competitive player, and Bill Russell was probably the greatest winner of all time.

**In your opinion, who are the top three leaders in the game today and why do you feel that way?**
I look at the thirty coaching jobs in the league as special – whoever is there is obviously a pretty darn good leader. A few other people stand out: Gregg Popovich, Bill Self and John Calipari. They all worked for me.

**In your opinion, who are the top three leaders in the world today and why do you feel that way?**
Tiger Woods is really special because I know how he affects so many people in a positive way. He's changed the game of golf. He's opened it up to minorities and young people. The U.S. Olympic Basketball Team that went to Spain in 1992 went to change our sport and made it global. They made our game better just by their participation – more or less what David Stern and everybody envisioned. My favorite leader, Jackie Robinson, is not around. I grew up in Brooklyn. I wound up walking pigeon-toed because of Jackie, and forty-two is a number that I'll always have a special place for. Because of what he endured and the effect he had on so many lives, he's memorable to me.

# Part 2:

# Leading from the Inside Out

# Chapter 5:

## The Secret Ingredient to Leadership: Self-Confidence

*"Excellence is the gradual result of <u>always</u> striving to do better."*

~Pat Riley

Possibly one of the most damaging and misleading myths about success circulating in the world today is that you will naturally become rich and successful if you just pick the thing that you love to do most and make it "your job,". We've all heard interviews with these people who all say that their journey to riches wasn't difficult because they loved what they do.

And in today's society where many people who want to get rich quick, it is for them to believe that doing what they love will turn them into a Jay-Z, Donald Trump or Sydney Poitier.

We all know that, regardless of who you are or whether or not you love what you do, becoming successful is NOT easy and requires a great deal of hard work and iniative. You will need to take the actions that every successful person does to become great. But here's the difference. Instead of scaring, threatening, or beating yourself into taking those actions, you will *naturally* want to do what you should do to become successful. If you are one of the lucky people who love what they do, then it will most likely be easier for you to be disciplined enough to do what it takes to become successful. But most people take this out of context when they think that becoming successful is a ride in the park. It isn't, no matter who you are or what you do.

I am sure the young Bill Gates would rather have been hanging out with his buddies as opposed to working in his garage at all hours of the day and night on his computer inventions. However he made this choice because he had a desire for success and a belief in what he was creating. There was something inside of him that helped him make the choice to focus on his work. That inner conviction, in fact, made it easy for Bill Gates to stay focused on his goals. Along with his self-confidence, he consistently made decisions from a place of faith in his abilities, and as a result became a very successful man. Someone who makes decisions from a place of fear would never have dropped out of a top college to tinker around in their garage 24/7.

**Just loving something is not enough to make you great or wealthy.**

Self confidence is the key to maintaining your drive and discipline to keep pushing ahead to reach your goals, even when your mind and body are at odds. There is something in you that makes you believe you are worth it. That your contribution counts. That you deserve the reward you will receive. This applies to basketball, parenting, running a business or any endeavor you are passionate about. You have to be able to make the decision to run drill after drill or project after project– even when you've just played a game the night before and you're physically wiped out. Self confidence and a belief in your ability, worth and contribution to your team will help you to work through rehabilitating an injury, burn the midnight oil to finish a business proposal, or sacrifice personal glory for the good of the team.

You will not be able to make the decisions that you need to make on a consistent basis if you are in it just because you enjoy it – regardless of how much you love what you do, there are parts of it that you will not love at all. Trust me, I love this game. I love to play. I love the smell of the court and the feeling I get in the pit of my stomach when I'm running down the court setting up a fast break. When that jersey slides over my head, I am alive in a special way. But, there are a lot of things that I *don't* love. For one, I don't love the physical pain of pushing your body to the absolute limit and beyond year after year after year. But, there is a secret that makes moving forward and getting up easier. That secret is trusting yourself to do it, day-in and day-out. From that trust comes the self-confidence to keep *on* doing it – even when fear, doubt and insecurity sneak in.

My dream was to play in the NBA, even though I initially wanted to play in the NFL like my older brother. I grew up in Canton, Ohio which was and still isa football town through and through. Basketball and baseball were just the things you did when you couldn't play football. As far as natural talent was concerned, I was much better at football than basketball. Since my older brother was drafted to play for the Kansas City Chiefs (thirteenth pick), football was very important for my family and just about every other family in Canton.

It seemed like most of the town would turn out for the games – even some of the away games. The pigskin was all I cared about, and for the first 15 years of my life I thought it was my first love. It wasn't until I was about 15 that I realized that football never held my attention the way basketball did. Football came so easily to m e, but I realized one day that all I liked about football was playing the games. I knew that this was an important realization, because I saw from my brother that being a professional football player was about 90% practice and 10% games. And I realized that I had a problem if the part I loved the most about the game wasn't the thing I would be doing the most.

Basketball, however, was another story. I loved everything about basketball: the feel of the ball in my hand, the sound of the shoes sliding on the floor, the strategy. I'd found something that I could do for the rest of my life – with passion. In football, I loved to play, but I disliked the practices, the weight lifting, and the fact that we only played one game a week. On the flipside, everything about basketball motivated me, practices included. As high school began and the football season approached, I began having my first doubts about that sport. I thought, *If I get injured and miss basketball, I'm going to be a little upset.* So I decided, then and there, I would rather prepare myself for something I had true passion for than play a game I was only partially into. That's a lesson I've tried to stick to throughout my life.

Listen to your heart. After making that decision, I never looked back. And I was lucky. I had the kind of supportive environment that gave me the confidence to choose a sport that I loved more, even though it wasn't as much of a "sure thing" for me.

I think that everyone faces that moment in life when he or she asks, *Do I take the sure thing, or do I go for what I truly love?* In my case, the respect and prestige I got from playing football dwarfed the personal response I had to basketball. I knew that a lifetime of football would not make me happy. Cheering from the stands, money nor pride would not change that. In my case, both options were risky. I don't know if that made it harder or easier to choose the even longer shot of pursuing a career in basketball or football.

For some people, the stakes are higher. They can join the family lumber mill business or they can pursue their dreams of opening a private investigative agency. They can go to law school or music school. They can open their own store or teach.

The risks are different for everyone. The stakes are different and the dream is different.

### But one thing that we all have in common is the fear that we will fail.

And the only way to combat that fear is with self-confidence. And the fear is real, no matter who you are or what you do.

The only way I know to combat that fear of failure is to surround yourself with positive people who believe in you. Having a vision that you believe in along with self-confidence definitely makes it more likely that you will have the drive to take *proactive action* which is how you will fulfill your dreams.

The first step, in a nutshell, is learning how to get what you want. And in order to do that, you have to have self-confidence. Not the artificial self-confidence that is based on how you look, how much money you have, or how intimidating you are. I'm talking about the self-confidence that makes you strong from the inside out – the kind of self-confidence that everyone wants because it is so magnetically attractive. I mean the kind of self-confidence that allows you to take risks because you are solid with yourself.

**Self-confidence is simply the ability to trust yourself to complete what you set your mind to accomplish.**

Here's the deal: we all make ourselves dozens of promises every day. They sound something like this: I will remember to pay the electric bill, call my mother, start working out, not eat junk food, stand up for myself, and so on. We create these to-do lists in our minds, but the bottom line is:

**Self-confident people keep the promisesthey make to themselves.**

The more promises you keep, the more you trust yourself. The more you trust yourself, the more confident you are. The more confident you are, the more likely you are to keep the promises that you make to yourself. So how do you build self-confidence from faith? Start keeping your promises to yourself; and when you have that nailed, keep those to others as well.

In this, like in many things, most people set themselves up to fail. We live in a society where people want what they want instantly: instant downloads, instant oatmeal, instant information. We are losing touch with the benefits of delayed gratification. Let's say that you make a promise to yourself to get in shape and you want to lose ten pounds. It takes a lot of work to do that, not to mention the discipline to eat right, stay focused and keep going to the gym when you don't feel like it. On top of that, we are trained to expect instant results. You might go to the gym for a few days, maybe even a week, but you don't see any results because this kind of thing takes months. So you quit. By doing that, you've broken trust with yourself. You now trust yourself less than you did before you started working out. The broken trust with yourself is *far* more damaging than not achieving the goal that you set.

So here are some tricks to help you win when it comes to building self-confidence:

1. **Set small, easily accomplished goals at first.** If you need to replace a light bulb that's been burned out for weeks in your bathroom, then make and keep that promise to yourself. Take out the trash when you say you will. These tiny things start to add up, and pretty soon, you'll find yourself taking on tasks and challenges that would have totally overwhelmed you before.

2. **Renegotiate your commitments.** If you make a commitment to yourself (or to others) that you simply won't be able to keep, don't just ignore it and break faith with everyone – including yourself. Renegotiate your commitments so that you can remain trustworthy in the eyes of others and yourself. I know it sounds strange to renegotiate with yourself, but ... your relationship *with you* is the most important one that you will ever have. If you can't trust yourself, or if you don't like yourself, there isn't a self-help book, a pill or a person that will be able to help you. WARNING: If you renegotiate your commitments, make certain that you follow through. You want be able to do this repeatedly and maintain the trust of those who depend on you.

3. **Celebrate your victories.** Oddly enough, we are conditioned to be negative and overly critical about ourselves. Remember the inner critic I mentioned earlier? Make it a point to listen to it less and celebrate your victories more! Your self confidence will grow tremendously if you do.

4. **Make decisions from a place of faith**. The best way to start building the confidence you need to excel at whatever you do is to start making your decisions from a place of faith. Trust me, trust great spiritual leaders, trust mentors, and trust coaches and start taking 100% responsibility for your life and your choices. It might be hard to do this at first, but as you start operating from a leadership mentality, you will see the most incredible things start to happen in your life. You will begin to trust yourself. As you trust yourself more, you will make even stronger and better choices – without as much effort. This is very important to understand, because not doing so will surely lead to low self-esteem. Low self-esteem or lack of confidence in yourself and abilities is simply the result of making a series of poor choices. You make a bad decision, and things go badly for you. Instead of realizing that the outcome was the result of your choices, you look outward to explain the problem. If you continue to make bad decisions and this behavior becomes becomea a habit, your self-confidence erodes and continues to do so until you become a chronic victim. A chronic victim is the antithesis of a leader. Please understand that a few bad decisions won't take you out of the game – allowing your self-confidence to erode and transform into low-self esteem will most certainly do so. Instead of making decsions from a place of faith in your self and your abilities, you now make them out of fear and a lack of trust in yourself. And success never comes from a place of fear.

If you can master these strategies, your self-confidence will grow and you will start to attract others to you like magnets. You will become an incredible leader because people will trust you and want to follow you. No tricks, no rapport-building gimmicks, no manipulative tactics to "make friends and influence people." Just honest, natural self-confidence that will lead to your success. And you will know what to tell the people that will start coming to you and asking how you did it.

## Self-Confident Leaders Acccept Radical Responsibility

One characteristic I believe all leaders share is their willingness to accept what I like to call "radical responsibility." The word *radical* means *extreme* or *departing from the usual*. To be *radically responsible* is to be extremely or unusually accountable, reliable, and dependable.

People who are radically responsible are the exact opposite of people who possess a victim mentality. Victims are very easy to spot. They constantly make excuses, pass the buck and shift blame onto everyone and everything except themselves. They can go through their entire lives avoiding responsibility. They are more focused on covering their backsides than they are in doing good work. We have all had our moments of avoiding blame and making excuses but, generally, people are willing to accept responsibility. Leaders, however, are willing to accept *radical* responsibility for themselves, their lives and their commitments.

Radical responsibility is the ability to be honest and objective as you look at situations and outcomes in your life and your role in them whether positive or negative. In a lot of ways, our society encourages us to be hard on ourselves. Being self-degrading is often mistaken for humility, while being honest about our strengths is often mistaken for arrogance. This way of thinking could not be more backwards or self-defeating. First of all, putting yourself down is never helpful. There is a big difference between being self-degrading and taking an honest look at what you could have done better.

It is similar to the difference between remorse and shame. Remorse is when you *know* that you have done something wrong. Shame is when you *feel* that you are wrong. Shame will eat away at your confidence like acid. Remorse, on the other hand, is an important part of being human. Acknowledging your wrong actions is a crucial part of growing into a better, more confident person, and a part of being a radically responsible leader. This does not mean that you need to make everything your fault. It means that you take full and total responsibility for everything that was within your power to affect. *Everything*.

## How You Do *Anything* is How You Do *Everything*

The *big* things in life are made up of the *little* things. No one just wakes up one day and becomes a top athlete, a successful businessperson, or a great parent. Becoming great at anything is just being great at a bunch of little things – slowly and over time.

If you want to be a professional ball player, then you have to excel at passing, dribbling, communicating with your teammates, giving feedback, shooting, running, and the list goes on. This is true for any endeavor. To become great, you must back up your desire and talent with skills. Learning skills takes time, discipline, and focus. Most importantly, it takes the mindset of a champion.

> **Champions know that how they do anything**
> **is how they do everything.**

I learned this best from Gary Payton. When I played with Gary and the Seattle SuperSonics, it didn't matter if he was at practice, in double overtime of a playoff series, or playing a pickup game with some buddies. When Gary was playing basketball, he was a champion at every moment. With true professional basketball players, I noticed that they weren't just champions on the court. You could see the champion mindset in how they lived their lives.

What these players have in common is the focus and determination they bring to everything they do – from running their community outreach programs to preparing for the playoffs.

How you do *anything* is how you do *everything*. Are you the kind of person who waits until the last minute and then rushes to get your work done? You know it could be better. You know you're not doing the job that you are capable of. Is that how you do everything – leaving it until the last minute and rushing through it? John Wooden often said something that comes to mind when I think of situations like this. He would ask, *"If you don't have time to do it right, then when will you have time to do it over?"* Can't argue with that one, can you?

Maybe you're the kind of person who gets overwhelmed by trying to make everything too good? You're anxious and frustrated, always demanding more from yourself and never finding the balance between drive and satisfaction. Do you always put others first, or do you put yourself first? Watch how your habits, your personality traits, and your idiosyncrasies play out across the board in your life.

People are funny about their own shortcomings. We have one of two reactions when those shortcomings are pointed out to us. We are either over-the-top hard on ourselves or we immediately minimize our shortcomings in our minds. Have you caught yourself doing that? You may say, "Yeah, *I know I interrupt! It's bad, but I'm working on it"* or, *"I know I'm anxious, but it's just the way I am. I'm not violent or mean."* Our faults appear so common that we just chalk them up to human nature. But the truth is shocking.

Please understand that your flaws are not small, insignificant things. They have a tremendous impact on your life and the lives of those around you and impact your life as strongly as water, oxygen, food and shelter in importance. Your flaws will cause you to rationalize yourself into a very mediocre life. Those little character defects that you have been hearing about your whole life are exactly what cause you to take the actions that you take – and the actions that you take determine the life that you will live.

# Chapter 6:

# Leaders Recognize the Power of the Team

*"I haven't seen one guy beat five people yet.*
*It needs to be done collectively."*

**~ Eric Snow**

Corporate teams are a lot like basketball teams; many personalities compete for a shot at the basket and, from time to time, star players – high performers – shine when they need to the most. However, the best team players and the highest performers are those that work in concert with everyone for the benefit of the team.

It's easy to look at the players with the highest scores and think they are the stars. However, consider who is working behind the scenes to make sure the "star" player is in line for an easy lay-up. Who motivates the team when everyone is down? Who is there for support, and who is the glue that binds the team together?

The true test of a fast, fluid and flexible leader is whether he or she can harness the power of their team; that is, can they give the star players room to move without forgetting the rest of the team of high performers and what they need – and want – to do their job behind the scenes even better.

## Hitting the Boards

If you scan the stats, you'll see that rebounds are not the strongest part of my individual game. That's what the score sheets say, anyway. As a six-foot three-inch tall guard, I don't typically rack up big numbers on the glass, but I can still play with the rebound-grabbing big guys.

As a leader on the floor, I preach team rebounding. I help the other four guys on the court focus as a group on snatching and securing those missed shots. Sure, your seven-footers are usually the guys who snare the ball as it clangs off the rim. *However, it is a team task.* It is a coordinated effort. It is crucial. Anybody who plays with me knows my three-part equation for basketball success:

**Low turnovers + low defensive shooting percentage**
**+ dominant rebounding usually = VICTORY**

It's that simple. When it comes to rebounding as a team, there are three essential elements: the plan to retake possession of the ball, the moment you go get it and, once you have it, the outlet pass that's needed to start your team's offense. In short: strategy, action, follow-through.

## Boxing Out

As players, we're taught this basic skill from the very beginning, usually the same day we're learning how to pass, dribble and shoot. When the other team launches a shot, you quickly muscle your way into position, commanding a spot between the man you are guarding and the basket. It's like a protective web with all five guys shielding the opposing team from the loose ball. Smaller players can be effective rebounders by using this technique against a bigger opponent. Positioning trumps body size.

When I remind my teammates that we have to rebound, what I'm really doing is promoting *collective responsibility.* This is a critical message for any leader: We win together and we lose together, in the small moments or in the big games or projects. We all own a piece of the outcome. We all have a duty. I haven't yet seen one guy beat five people. It needs to be done collectively.

To build collective responsibility, a leader first must get buy-in from his team. Everyone must agree on the mission and the goal. You come to consensus on what is appropriate and what's not. When you set expectations as a team, there's more accountability for people when they don't live up to their own duties. Guilt is a prime motivational tool. If I must answer to fourteen other players, I am motivated to my very best. Failure also brings collective guilt and collective disappointment. Simply put, it hurts to let the group down.

Once you have the mission or the goal in place, it helps if you can get public acknowledgement from the team: *Yes, we're all going to show up. We're all going to do our part.* In my world it may be, *Yes, we're all going to box out.* That public agreement forms a sort of pact or a verbal contract between each of the players. You're there for each other, and you all know it. By publicly declaring it, you also form a contract between you and your own integrity.

Yes, there are dozens of big, hulking centers and power forwards in the NBA who sign multi-million dollar contracts because they post sparkling rebounding numbers. There is no question these players receive a lot of the glory. However, those same players also understand that their teammates pitched in to get the job done. In other words, the only thing that matters is the team.

So what do you do when you have players who won't chip in or pull their weight? What happens when guys would rather dash to the other end of the court – looking for the long outlet pass and the subsequent dunk – rather than choosing to stay back to help the team box out, do the dirty work and secure the rebound? How do you handle a lone wolf? How do you call people out on the court on in the boardroom?

This is one of the most delicate acts of leadership. Every person is unique. Every personality is distinct. Different players have their own ways of accepting, hearing and absorbing criticism. Long before you come down on someone as a leader, you should first try to establish and build a relationship with that person. Tell them that when you are pointing out things they could have done better, you have their best interest – and the team's interests – uppermost in your mind. Then people know they can trust your judgment. They will be more open to your critiques.

Once that rapport is in place, you have to be able to read people. You have to truly know their character. Are they the types that can handle criticism only when it's delivered one-on-one? Are they more apt to respond if you challenge them in front of the team? Choosing the proper critical words – and the right place and time to deliver them – is truly a craft and one you will need to perfect if you want to be authentic and helpful to someone.

Anybody can dispense discipline. Anybody can yell. Real leadership does not mean dictatorship. What you really want are positive results. And that generally takes a careful blend of firmness and friendliness. If I see a sensitive personal issue occurring with a player, I deal with it – and him – in private. If a player is failing in some part of his game or is hurting the team on or off the court, then I make it a team thing.

When speaking as the team captain – or just talking teammate to teammate – I'm always truthful and sometimes maybe even a bit blunt. Even at Michigan State, my teammates considered me brutally honest. However, if I saw the need to correct, inspire or call out a teammate, I stayed mindful of that teammate's particular personality.

I believe that I developed and still maintain a heightened awareness of the feelings of my teammates during my college years. Now, some of my closest Michigan State friends say I had the soul of an army sergeant during the games or even at practice. If I had barked or hollered, I would remember the exact message I delivered in the heat of the moment and would go back to that player and put things right if I felt I had upset them.

Some leaders get caught up in the battle and say some harsh things to achieve a victory or success. They neglect to deal with the human response, the backlash of that take-charge attitude. Sometimes feelings get hurt or people don't understand the reasons for the outburst. I made it a practice to later explain to my teammates why I did or said certain things in a critical moment. In turn, they trusted me and trusted what I said. They did not take my criticism personally because they understood the motives behind my spirited instructions – to see us improve as a team.

I tried to never forget the team's emotional needs. After a game, I would rewind the tape in my mind and recall exactly what I said and how I had led, and then I would ask myself: "What could I do better the next time?" That attention to detail and care for a teammate's state of mind always makes a leader better.

I can think of at least two NBA coaches who have that innate ability to be tough yet understanding, and can effectively read playrs and tailor their messages to him. They are Gregg Popovich, the head coach of the San Antonio Spurs, and Larry Brown, now the head coach in Charlotte. They can effortlessly straddle those two worlds and act as a disciplinarian when the time is right and a mentor when a softer touch is needed. To me, that's the mark of a strong leader. "Pop" – as we call Gregg Popovich in the NBA – probably learned that flexibility while working as a volunteer assistant on Larry Brown's staff at the University of Kansas.

So, let's talk about how this relates to the art of rebounding. Let's say my speech to the team to shore up our group rebounding has paid off. We have come together and we are controlling the boards night in and night out. Let's say it has even become our trademark and our edge, giving us more possessions and, ultimately, more wins. How do I maintain that collective responsibility?

The leader must be the one who stands up and acts – not just when there's adversity, but also when things are going well to keep that positive momentum flowing and to reinforce good team habits. A leader has to be the person who sets the example and the expectation that the collective responsibility will stay strong. The leader proves that the strong work ethic and new strategies are in place to stay.

There are always potential cracks in that foundation. Mistakes happen. Humans are human. Bad habits return and responsibilities are shirked. If the leader has established the proper culture, these setbacks will prompt other people – especially those lower on the chain of command – to jump in and take action whenever they see a colleague break ranks. If a leader has created a healthy team environment, there will be watchdogs everywhere making sure nobody disrupts the group's success. Total buy-in has been achieved.

A leader can't be everywhere and can't notice every flaw that occurs. Besides, you don't want to micromanage. You often have to rely on other people to bring problems to your attention. That's why an open-door policy is vital. It is so important for the people around you to feel they can trust you and can talk to you openly and confidentially.

Here is the key: if concerns arise, a leader can never ignore them. He must react swiftly, even if the complaint is unwarranted or if the reported issue appears unimportant. A high level of responsiveness is essential.

You want all the eyes and ears on the team looking and listening for problems. It bolsters morale, and when a leader looks into these reported matters and thanks people for having the courage to come forward – even if the grievance wasn't valid – it reinforces the fact that you have their back. When complaints fall on deaf ears at the top, it can be more debilitating and damaging to team culture than the original complaint itself.

## Looking For the Outlet

So, let's say all the hard work has paid off in a momentary success. You and your teammates boxed out their men and you have snared the rebound. Now you are instantly surrounded by a forest of opposing players who are swatting at the ball and yanking at what you have. The competition is closing in.

It's time to look up court, peer through all the fierce physical traffic and find an open teammate to whom to pass the ball. That will trigger a fast break or be the spark for launching the half-court offense. This will jump start your team. It begins with making that first connection and figuring out a way to collaborate. You must swiftly analyze the situation and choose your next move.

Leadership requires you to always look ahead and to have a line of attack for your team to follow. At the same time, you must be able to adjust on the fly and react to circumstances in front of you. Leaders train their people to think three steps in the future, and then to come up with an array of contingencies in case the future you imagined suddenly crumbles into some new reality.

Let's say I'm trying to make that outlet pass, and my first instinct is to find and connect with LeBron James. This *was* my plan, but I see that he's covered by two defenders. *Contingency time.* Immediately, I look for an open teammate, and I spot Wally Szczerbiak standing alone near our free throw line. I toss the ball to Wally, he makes two dribbles and dunks.

I consider myself something of a cerebral player. I think other people on my team and around the league see me that way, too. I pride myself on how I have studied the sport and have taught myself how to understand where a game might be headed next. This is where experience meets anticipation.

For example, if we're running a set play and I see the defenders are overplaying – aggressively cheating into the passing lanes and crowding my guys – I know that the next time we have the ball, we'll have a golden opportunity to take advantage of that assertive defensive style. I tell one of my teammates what I'm thinking.

Twenty seconds later I get the ball again. I have that same teammate make one step toward me – as if he's looking for a pass – then plant and dart behind his defender toward the basket. That defender is caught out of position, leaning the wrong way, and the cutter is wide open to hit for a lay-up. You know this play as "The Back Door. In that case, I have recognized a weakness in the moment, something to exploit, and then flashed forward to concoct a way to seize the advantage.

During my time with the Philadelphia 76ers, Allen Iverson and I had an intangible, unspoken ability to each see the game a few steps ahead and to both know what we were going to do next and to manipulate whatever the defense was doing. I would move my eyes or nod my head and he would instantly know what I was thinking: *Next time down the court, go back door.* He got a lot of lay-ups that way – and I got a lot of assists.

Nonverbal communication of this kind is as important as an intimate, one-on-one chat or a group discussion. Sometimes you need to be able to relay your message in a glance or a look, maybe during a meeting between your team and a client. But, you also don't want to give people mixed messages or the wrong idea about what you are thinking. What you say through body language and facial expressions can be vital and should be clear. As a leader, you should be able to read body language, too – in posture, tone, and inflection, through eye contact and by being plugged in to people.

In the workplace, deciphering nonverbal communication takes something called "emotional recognition." This is the ability to be aware of other people's emotions, and specifically what's going on below the surface.

According to HelpGuide.org, having this kind of emotional savvy allows you to:

- **"Accurately read the emotional cues others send** —pick up on worry, sadness, grief, or feelings of being overwhelmed.

- **Respond with nonverbal cues that reflect emotional understanding and care** —indicating that you notice and care.

- **Be congruent** — avoid confusing and confounding others with words that contradict your true feelings.

- **Know if the relationship is meeting your emotional needs** — giving you the ability to repair the relationship or move on."

Now, it's a long way from that level of expertise and, say, making eye contact on the court with Allen Iverson, but at the core of both is the valuable art of reading human cues and using that information.

Messages come in all forms and in all volumes. A good leader listens to everything … like when other players are shouting for the ball. This takes us back to that post-rebound outlet pass. To me, there are some larger lessons packed into that brief moment of a basketball game – ethics that transcend sports and are useful in the business world. Here's why: If I'm looking to make an outlet pass, my teammates are expected to come toward me, to get open, to call for the ball when they are open and to shorten the distance between us.

This is the essence of an alliance – on the court and in the workplace. Just like that, we're back to that theme of collective responsibility. Teammates and colleagues need to give feedback about where they are and where they are going next. The leader – the guy with the ball – must be watching and listening for the message.

Even if you don't have the ball – even if the responsibility isn't currently in your hands – it's still your job to pay attention and move toward your partners so you can lend a hand. You must shorten the distance between you and your teammate to complete the task. If a leader has fostered loyalty, this is where it pays off.

## Leaders Model Commitment for their Teams

Through years of leadership, my teammates knew how much I valued the game, so they never doubted my commitment. I gained their respect by respecting them and by treating them the way I would want to be treated. They knew what I stood for and how much I cared.

When you establish that kind of personal stronghold with people, it takes away any questions about your ability to continue contributing to the team's cause.

Before injuries took a toll on my body, I was usually the first one on the court for practice and the last to leave. I think this is one of the reasons leadership is so tough for many people: you have to represent whatever it is you want to convey. If you think your team needs to devote more time to practicing defense or free throws, you had better be out there on the practice floor doing that yourself.

After years of wear and tear on my body, I couldn't be the first guy on and the last guy off the court anymore. I had to rest more to be ready for game time. I never complained or made a big issue of my injuries, but the list included: a broken right ankle (I have a plate and seven screws in there), a broken left thumb (I have a plate and five screws in there), and a torn meniscus in my left knee. As these injuries mounted, they slowed me down. And when my teammates saw the difference in my body and my pace, they instinctively knew I was hurt.

At the same time, playing hurt can be a good opportunity to lead by example. A leader doesn't have to pretend that putting in extra work – or that toiling through a painful time – is fun.

There's nothing joyful about, say, coming to work on Saturday because a project demands it. A leader shouldn't paste on a fake smile and pretend everything is perfect. But by showing up, you can illustrate that you are willing to work even when you don't feel like it. That attitude becomes infectious. (That's also why it's crucial to call out people when they are being lazy. That kind of behavior can be contagious, too.)

When the injuries began to stack up, I wasn't as quick or nimble as I was in my rookie days. A good leader will admit: *I'm not perfect. We're all just human. We're all struggling, trying to get better.* It's a message of solidarity and one that shows commitment.

In the old leadership model, the person at the top projected a certain image of perfection or a notion that he or she was special. This type of behavior tended to create more distance between people. Folks in the trenches felt they couldn't match that type of perfection. But there is strength in being authentic and in being real. It promotes a sense of collective vulnerability. It says, *We will get through the tough times together.* If I ever need a personal example to share with my team, I could tell them about my struggles to run long distance on a Michigan State track. That's a truly humbling story.

On the basketball court, I could fly. Even when we did 100-meter training sprints, I always led the pack. But every pre-season, during a mandatory team run we called "the Spartan Mile," I faltered. Before we began, Coach Heathcote established our minimum times for finishing the race. Guards were given fewer minutes than the big guys to complete the distance. I never made my allotted time. And as a penalty, Coach made me repeat the entire run. During my final, exhausted lap around the track, some teammates joined me and pushed me to cut my time. In that moment, we all pulled together.

Many traits go into a leader's ability to create that larger sense of group responsibility and commitment to the team. It's not only the capacity to respond to challenges; it's the knack for publicly sharing your own struggle. It's as if you are saying, "I understand that this is hard. I'm right there with you."

There's nothing worse than a leader who doesn't live up to a commitment or who doesn't follow through. Those who routinely fail to follow through lack integrity. That lack of integrity can be like a splinter in your finger: a little bothersome at first but over time it starts to fester. Through your actions and your work ethic, however, you can set the bar high for the rest of the team. Good habits are contagious, and so is the drive to be committed to your team and its success.

## Thoughts on Leadership by Nate McMillan, Head Coach of the Portland Trail Blazers

**What are the top three qualities of a good leader?**

A good leader has to be prepared, organized and able to communicate.

**What are the top three faults of a bad leader?**

If you're not prepared, you can't lead anyone. You're basically going into a situation blindly. If you're not organized I don't think you can lead anyone, because everything becomes a surprise. If you can't communicate what you want to do, what you want your group to believe in, they won't follow you.

**Who are or were the three most important leaders in your life and why?**

My mother Jeanette had to work for everything she had. She raised six kids as a single parent. She just taught us the values, the important things in life: that you have to work hard at whatever you do and respect others. Basically, do the right thing and use common sense in your decisions. My older brother Randy was a father figure. There was no father in our family. My mother had to stop school in the seventh grade, but Randy went on to graduate and got a scholarship, got his degree and set the example for his younger brothers. My coaches were very important, too. It started with my little league coach. But I would list the entire coaching fraternity.

**In your opinion, who were the three top leaders in NBA history and why do you feel that way?**

Commissioner David Stern has basically taken the NBA in a different direction and it is now definitely one of the top sports professions in our country. There's Magic Johnson and Larry Bird. I started watching basketball only when they came into the league. Those guys and Julius "Dr. J" Erving helped the NBA go to another level, really motivated people and became role models. They were people that a lot of players wanted to be like.

**In your opinion, who are the top three leaders in the league today and why do you feel that way?**
As the commissioner of the association, David Stern has overseen its growth over the past twenty-four years. This growth included the introduction of the WNBA and more. Jerry Colangelo (former owner of the Suns, current head of USA Basketball) gave a lot to the league and is someone whose opinions are valued by Commissioner Stern. I admire Pat Riley because he works to make the league better.

**In your opinion, who are the top leaders in the world today and why do you feel that way?** Barack Obama is my first pick. His commitment to the people of this country is honorable. Bill Gates has had a huge impact on America through the things his technology has done for the country and for the world. He is huge.

# Chapter 7:

# Becoming a Highly Effective Leader in Today's REAL World

*"It's what you learn after you know it all that counts."*

**~Unknown**

L ook around at your life. If you are the best at everything you do, then you need to get some new friends or step outside your comfort zone. It is far better to be the worst player on the best team than the best player on the worst team. Why? Because being around people who are better than you will pull you up. You will get better just by being around them – by playing at their level.

But it works the other way, too. If people who aren't as talented as you constantly surround you, you will stay where you are – or maybe even slip a little.

If it is your goal to be a success at whatever you do – and to even go a step further and be a *leader* at what you do – then reaching farther, digging down deeper, expanding your comfort zone, growing and changing, improving your abilities ... these will have to become necessities in your daily walk. I appreciate what Pastor Steve Robinson of Church of the King Church in Mandeville, LA, says about growth and change: "Anything that is alive is growing. Anything that is growing is changing. Anything growing and changing is healthy!"

This book is about helping you become a fast, fluid and flexible leader. In this section, I want to help you create a more solid foundation on which to lead quickly, if not instantaneously. My *Four Pillars of Leadership Success* will show you how to improve your leadership abilities and give you more guidance around leading high performers in our rapidly changing business environment.

## Becoming a Fast Leader - Speed Works!

Speed is absolutely essential when leading those at the top of their game. Regardless of whether or not they are born performers, created rock stars or consummate professionals who never slow down, for anybody, your ability to get up to speed, stay there and, in fact, surpass your high performers whenever possible (to stay one step ahead) is critical to your success.

But speed does not happen on its own, and many leaders of high performers don't naturally work at such fast peaces themselves. As such you must build a solid foundation so that every new high performer, situation, challenge or mission is a blank slate. The more solid your foundation, the more quickly you adapt to new situations and the more promptly you can respond to your high performer's needs. Here are my **Four Pillars of Leadership Success** that will help you build this foundation:

- **The First Pillar:** Here, the leader is asked to review his or her leadership background. How did they get to where they are now? What skills do they bring to this critical mission? These are important reflections on how they developed their leadership skills, who helped them discover and, later, develop their leadership skills, recalling experiences with success as a leader, remembering that most leaders were themselves at one time high performers (stars).

- **The Second Pillar:** This section is all about understanding the high performers (stars). What are the characteristics that high performers generally share that have helped them become successful? Reviewing their previous work methodology to ascertain how they have become successful will create a backlog of understanding that will help you lead them.

- **The Third Pillar:** Here the leader develops specific strategies and a "game plan" to fit the high achiever(s). This pillar of their leadership foundation is critical to working quickly and effectively; this game plan actively facilitates speed on behalf of the leader. Team and organizational goals are assessed and are an integral part of putting together this game plan.

- **The Fourth Pillar:** Here, support for the leader and what that looks like from within the organization is determined. Does the organization provide the backing that a leader may need to be effective in influencing high performers? Leaders are not alone in this venture and must not only identify their support system but actively involve them in the fast, decisive leadership that is so critical to the organization.

## Additional Strategies to Increase Your Effectiveness as a Leader

### Strategy 1: Time Management

Time is the most valuable commodity you have. You can't buy it, hoard it, borrow it or get more of it. Yet, what you do with it determines what you get out of life. How you handle your time makes the difference between success and failure, happiness and sadness, being overwhelmed or being confident. Perhaps the scariest thing about time is its ability to create a state of panic.

When you get overwhelmed with the tasks that need to be accomplished, or when you start to feel that there simply isn't enough time to handle them all, you start to panic. That or you go into denial.

Neither of these reactions is useful.. Panic can undermine your efforts to become successful very quickly. There's one simple reason: You start to cut corners. You lose the powerful attitude of doing your very best at every moment, and you begin to rationalize the mindset that has you do everything as quickly as possible just to be able to cross it off your list..

There is a simple way to eliminate panic from your life – once and for all. I learned this from Coach Tom Izzo.

I was in college, playing basketball and was the punch line of the favorite national sports jokes. I worked overtime to fix my free throw problems while taking a full load of college classes. I had no time. I was starting to resent the hours that I slept every night because I could have used them for something more productive. I was headed for a panic that could have ended my career before it ever started. Had my coach not taken me aside and given me some of the best advice I've ever gotten, it would have been over. He said, "Eric, there is one infallible solution to being overwhelmed that will work every time. It is the ability to prioritize."

Instead of trying to get me to follow a complicated time-management schedule that had worked for him when he played college ball or trying to make me more productive when I was already in an unproductive state, he taught me how to prioritize. That gave me the ability to set my own schedule and keep it because it made sense to me.

It's really simple, and I still use it today. Every night I make a list of all the things that I want to accomplish the following day. Then I take my pen and put a number next to the six most important tasks, ranking them in order of priority – one being the most important, two being the second most important and so on. The next day, I simply start with the first task on my list and work on it until it is done to the best of my ability. Then I work on number two and so on.

One of the reasons that this works for me and for so many people is that it takes into account that priorities change, sometimes on a daily basis. For example, when my son got sick, taking care of him became the number one task on my list. This is so powerful, because it works in tandem with the concepts behind building self-confidence. It is just another way to make sure that you are keeping your promises to yourself.

If I want to be a better father, and I can see that I made my sons a priority in my life by consistently following through on the actions that I have promised myself I would take, then I believe myself when I see evidence that I am a better father. That then builds more confidence, which makes it easier for me to be a better person, father and leader.

Contrast that with the typical way of doing things. We promise ourselves that we are going to be better parents – and we try. We *try* to make their games a priority, or we *try* to help them with homework, but because our minds are on the 101 other things that are nagging at us, we aren't fully present for the children. Then, what if you know that you didn't do the best possible job you could have done as parents – even if, technically, you "put in the time." That's the real killer. You might be able to fool others for awhile, but you can't fool yourself. You know when you have done your best, and you know when you haven't.

By simply making a list of priorities and sticking to them, you can do your best without the sense that you should be doing something else. The task at hand has your full and focused attention. That makes it easy to do your very best in every situation. This will then lead to some extraordinary results in your life – from parenting, to playing in the NBA, to becoming a millionaire business owner or a champion quilter.

It all starts with the ability to manage your time – and your attitude. Here's an example of my schedule:

| | MON | TUE | WED | THU | FRI | SAT | SUN |
|---|---|---|---|---|---|---|---|
| 7-8 | Prepare Kids for School Breakfast | Prepare Kids for School Breakfast | Call kids prepare for school | Call kids prepare for school | Prepare kids for School Breakfast | Prepare kids for School Breakfast | Prepare kids for church Breakfast |
| 8-9 | Take Kids to School | Take Kids to School | Team Breakfast Mtg | Team Breakfast Mtg | Take kids to school | Attend Kids team sporting event | Attend service |
| 9-10 | Head to arena pre-game practice | Travel to Practice Facility | Therapy | Therapy Morning phone interview | Head to arena for therapy | Attend Kids team sporting event | Drive to arena pre-game practice |
| 10-11 | Shootaround | Practice Therapy | Board Bus for Team Practice | Board Bus for Team Practice Shootaround | Mtg with trainers | Attend Kids team sporting event | Pre-Game stretch. weights |
| 11-12 | -----11:15----- Practice | | -----11:15-- Team Practice | | -----11:15----- Light practice | Therapy Team Film | Pre-Game Mtg/media |
| 12-1 | -----12:30----- Drive home | Film/Team Mtg/Practice | -----12:30----- | Team Film Session | -----12:30----- Team Mtg | Light Practice | Pre-Game warm-up team chapel |
| 1-2 | -----1:45----- | Extra Court time with Asst. Coaches | Team Film Session | Team Luncheon | -----1:45----- | Foundation Community Appearance | HOME GAME |
| 2-3 | Pre-Game Rest | Pack for Road Trip/Head to Airport for | Lunch w/business associates | Pre-Game NAP | Team Autograph signing | Foundation Community Appearance | HOME GAME |
| 3-4 | Drive to arena – radio call in | | Pre-Game NAP | | Head Home | Head home from appearance | GAME-post game media weights & treatment |
| 4-5 | Pre-Game stretch. weights. massage | Flight to New City for Road Game | Call Kids and Leave Hotel and Board Bus for arena | Call kids handle family & business affairs | Play time w/kids or after school activity | Kids playtime NAP | Post game meal/family leave arena |
| 5-6 | Pre-Game Meal. pre-game TV interview | Flight | Pre-Game Media interview therapy | Leave Hotel and Board Bus for arena later game | Kids homework | NAP | Arrive home |
| 6-7 | Pre-Game warm-up w/coaches & team chapel | Flight Arrive in New City | Pre-Game warm-up Light Snack team chapel | Pre-Game meal/therapy radio/TV interview | Family Dinner | Family Activity | Kids Playtime |
| 7-8 | HOME GAME | Dinner with personal business partners | AWAY GAME | Pre-Game warm-up Light Snack team chapel | Team Community Relations Appearance | Family Activity | Kids Playtime |
| 8-9 | HOME GAME | Physical Therapy | AWAY GAME | AWAY GAME | Put kids to bed | Late business meeting | Put kids to bed |
| 9-10 | GAME-post game media weights & treatment | Return calls. emails. review film/game notes | Postgame media therapy treatment | AWAY GAME | Return business calls. emails. letters | Late business meeting | Therapy return business calls. emails |
| 10-11 | post game meal/family leave arena | Call home/TV | Head to airport from arena | GAME/post game media call home | Therapy | Put kids to bed | Watch TV read |
| 11-12 | Arrive home get kids into bed rest sleep | Read/Sleep | Depart for New City | head to airport arrive home at 3am | Rest/Sleep | Rest/Sleep | Rest/Sleep |

Because you prioritized your tasks, you will have done the most important things first. The smaller tasks can wait. Because you weren't trying to rush through your tasks to get rid of the nagging, overwhelming cloud above your head, you did everything with extraordinary care.

## Strategy 2: Handling Pressure

Having a high tolerance *for stress and pressure* comes from having put in the time and effort to become great at every aspect of your job or your team goal. When you know what needs to be done from every position to get to the goal, *then* you can function in environments that would be far too harrowing for someone with less experience and knowledge.

Imagine if you received a call to be the safety checker on an airline's international flights. It will be your job to release every plane for overseas travel. This is a highly stressful job with very high stakes; hundreds of thousands of people would be depending on you to keep them safe.

How well do you think you would be able to handle the stress if you knew very little about your job? My guess is not too well. I know I'd be freaking out a little. But, if you were confident in the knowledge that you had learned absolutely everything there was to know about overseas airline safety and that you were, by far, the single most qualified person for the job, would that have an effect on your ability to handle the stress and pressure? If you believeyou are the best person for the job, the stress and pressure would fade into a *certainty* that you *could* perform the task at hand. It is the same with every other job in the world – from playing basketball, to running a business to deploying troops. Therefore, it is *your* responsibility to become the very best at whatever you do. It is *your* responsibility to your teammates and to yourself to be equipped to succeed at your job.

There is still stress and pressure, but there is the sure and certain understanding that you did your absolute best work possible – in *that* moment and in *all* the moments leading up to it. If you know without a shadow of a doubt that you did all that you could do – whether you win or lose, succeed or fail – you will live a happy, contended, peaceful life. You will be able to handle jobs and positions that would have most people running away in terror.

## Strategy 3: Handling Risk

Leaders absolutely must have a high tolerance for risk. This isn't something you learn to endure like plunging yourself into ice-cold water to develop a tolerance to freezing temperatures. Instead, a high risk tolerance should evolve *naturally* from the ability to keep the big picture in mind and, therefore, have the ability to see mistakes as feedback rather than failure. It is a naturally evolving process that involves developing tolerance by repeated exposure to risky things.

## Strategy 4: Resilience

*"Adversity doesn't necessarily* create *character, but it certainly* reveals *it." ~ Unknown*

Adversity does create *resilience*. If you want to know yourself, don't look in the mirror on a bright sunny day when everything is going your way. The philosopher Horace says, "Misfortunes, untoward events lay open and disclose the skill of a general, while success conceals his weakness, his weak points." Maybe it's the day you get the parking ticket and your car gets towed. Or the day you get in a fight with your spouse before work. Or the day you have to do a one-day trip for work from LA to New York. To find out where you have room to grow, watch what happens to you under stressful circumstances. When do you snap at your spouse? Is it over money? Time? Your mother-in-law?

Watch your reactions when you have a bad day. It will show you where your challenges are as a leader. And it will give you the most critical element for effective leadership: compassion. As Martin Luther King, Jr. said, "The ultimate measure of a man is not where he stands in moments of comfort, but where he stands at times of challenge and controversy."

## Thoughts on Leadership by LeBron James, Cleveland Cavaliers

**What are the top three qualities of a good leader?**
A good leader leads by example, helps people succeed and gives them what they need to get the job done. He steps up to the challenge and does what it takes to win, even if it means doing the heavy lifting. He never forgets where he came from and gives back to the community by taking care of people who need help.

**Who are or were the three most important leaders in your life and why?**
My mom, Gloria James, taught me how to be a good person both on and off the court. Frankie Walker, one of my childhood coaches and mentors, helped me understand that I had to take responsibility for my actions. Dru Joyce II (coach of St. Vincent-St. Mary) taught me the skills and sportsmanship I needed to play basketball at a high level.

**In your opinion, who were the three top leaders in NBA history and why do you feel that way?**
There's Michael Jordan who never gave up and was always focused on winning. Oscar Robertson was the ultimate playmaker, and Magic Johnson knew how to let everyone around him enjoy the spoils of his talent.

**In your opinion, who are the top three leaders in the league today and why do you feel that way?**
Kobe Bryant knows how to raise his game to the highest level. Chris Paul is a great leader who motivates his teammates and thrives under pressure, and Kevin Garnett brings his undeniable attitude to his teammates, coaches, fans and everyone around him.

**In your opinion, who are the top leaders in the world today and why do you feel that way?**
Nelson Mandela never lost hope, despite his situation, and is an inspiration to everyone. Muhammad Ali always believed what he was doing was right and never backed down from anyone or anything.

# Chapter 8
# Your Best Defense

*"Life is not a spectator sport. If you're going to spend your whole life in the grandstand just watching, then you're wasting your life."*

~ Jackie Robinson

Defense wins basketball games. Defense also helped keep me in the NBA for over a decade and has helped shaped my leadership style. In college and throughout my pro career, I made it my craft. I studied, worked and executed on defense. After the 2002-2003 season, I was named to the All-NBA Defensive Second Team while playing for the 76ers. That is an honor I will always cherish. To make it, you must be voted in by the thirty NBA coaches, and the coaches are not allowed to vote for players on their own teams.

Here's the thing about defense: with the right skills and heart, you can contain, shut down and even dominate bigger players. Sure, height matters. It can be far harder for me to guard a six-foot, nine-inch forward than a six-foot, four inch guard. But in the NBA, you're constantly forced to take on bigger players – by design or through switches – and you just have to do your job. Handling the "bigs" never intimidated me. Size is never an excuse.

Check out the list of NBA Defensive Player of the Year winners. On that select, historic list, you'll see guards like Gary Payton (six foot four), Alvin Robertson and Sidney Moncrief (both six foot three, like me). I reveled in the chance to defend opponents who were taller or thicker, stronger or quicker. I knew I was helping my teammates if I took a major chunk of the defensive load, maybe by guarding one of the other team's forwards. Plus, I was good at it.

**A leader always wants to show his team he
can stand up to the tallest challenges.**

Playing solid defense combines intellect, willpower and physical skill. You are often required to out-think, out-hustle, and out-muscle your opponent.

Preparation is everything. You have to do your homework. Anticipation and instinct are as indispensable as quick feet and fast hands. In other words, the same gifts that make a player a great defender are talents that can take him places in life.

## Big Man or Big Moment: Don't Back Down

In writing this book – especially this chapter – I had to mull this question: What makes me a good NBA defender? Number one is the will. The will and the want-to.

I bask in the moments when I can take on the great scorers, and when I can pass the toughest tests. I don't run from problems. I embrace them. Give me twenty-five minutes against Allen Iverson or Kobe Bryant. After the game, I'll be exhausted. I may even be frustrated by their vast skills with the ball. But I'll have enjoyed the on-court tussle.

Successful nights usually mean I've caused the man I'm guarding to take more shots than normal – and tougher shots – to get his points. Again, a low shooting percentage for the other team means my guys are getting more opportunities to score. Making the opponent miss often triggers our fast break – an easier way to score baskets because the defense usually isn't in the proper position to stop you.

Having that *want-to* also means I've had the resolve during my career to sit down and study the personnel we're playing against and to learn their strengths and weaknesses. A good defender tries to force an offensive player to use the weakest parts of his game – like positioning your body in a way that makes a right-handed player dribble to his left. You have to watch film, analyze the games and search for those Achilles' heels to exploit.

Larry Brown has often praised my knack for coercing an opposing player to do things with the ball that he didn't want to do or wasn't comfortable doing. When playing against the big guys – or facing the big moments in life – it's natural to be nervous, scared, unsure or even intimidated. This is the way we're wired. It's our survival instinct: fight or flight.

One way to battle those demons and to change that mindset is to have a strong sense of the reason behind your mission. Say my assignment is to guard Detroit's Chauncey Billups, who can shoot well from outside and is equally effective driving to the hoop. That's a grueling job for me, but here's my thought process before the game: *If I can make it tough for Chauncey tonight, we'll have a greater opportunity to win.*

A compelling vision can overshadow the fear, can reduce the intimidation factor and can give you strength. Having a solid *why* will take care of the *how.* This is how you lead among giants if you're not a giant yourself – if you're not a superstar. This is how you walk into a room and own the moment. Use the challenge to boost your energy and to motivate yourself rather than being intimidated by it. In three words: bring it on.

Few people I know have faced a bigger challenge in life than my college teammate Shawn Respert. Shawn was the shooting guard at Michigan State when I played point guard. We were an electric backcourt tandem, not to mention tight friends.

Shawn was a prolific scorer, averaging 25.6 points per game as a senior and making the All-American first team. Portland used the eighth overall pick in the 1995 NBA Draft to select Shawn although he was immediately traded to Milwaukee. Toward the end of his rookie season with the Bucks, he began having stomach pains. Soon, he felt a marble-sized lump on his abdomen and went to see a doctor. In May 1996, he was diagnosed with stomach cancer. He was 23.

Shawn got daily radiation treatments to kill the cancer, and those went on for three months. Next, his doctors added even more radiation and some medicine to improve his chances. He lost twenty pounds. The only people he told were the Bucks' trainers, doctors and his head coach and general manager, Mike Dunleavy. He didn't mention the illness to his girlfriend, parents or grandparents.

With his NBA scoring average sputtering at about 5 points per game, the press began labeling Shawn as a high-draft bust, but he never complained or used the cancer as an excuse.

He understood his illness would have made a great media story and would have drawn sympathy, but at the end of the day, he knew he had to handle it himself. He used the setback to become an even a better man.

He even participated in a basketball summer league in 1996 in the midst of his treatment. The cancer was eventually cured and Shawn later played another three seasons in the NBA.

Shawn later confided in me that he had learned a few lessons from me in college that helped him manage the cancer ordeal. He discovered how to take something catastrophic and turn it into a positive, how to deal with it mentally and take a businesslike approach. He realized that he didn't need to cry about it – these were simply the cards had had been dealt.

He also said that watching me deal with the media also helped him deal with the publicly misunderstood decline in his basketball skills. He remembered how I fended off people who attacked me as a player or as a person while at Michigan State. He had seen how I used those challenges to motivate me to be better, to make it in the NBA.

In crisis, what makes one person a victim and another a victor? It's all in how you react. When in a tough spot, victors use a different language. Confronted with a sudden problem or a potential disaster, it's normal for the first reaction to be: *Oh my God! How am I going to deal with this?* Victims often get stuck there. They can't move past that panic.

Victors see the same scenario, ask the same question, and decide to conquer the moment – in whatever way they can. Their internal conversation sounds like this: "This adversary has no idea what it's about to face." Or, in basketball terms, "This big guy is about to get schooled." So many times confidence begins with those internal conversations. If I'm covering a guy who has me by five inches and fifty pounds, do I say, "Uh-oh"? No. I say, "This guy has no clue what's in store for him. This is my night."

A successful leader inspires himself with that kind of positive self-talk. Be your own coach. Control your thoughts. Don't let your thoughts control you. Beating the odds even once makes you more confident the next time you're tested. Do it again, and confidence becomes an everyday habit.

What is your focus? When life gets rocky, do you see obstacles or do you see opportunity? The only difference is how a person uses that misfortune or that uphill battle to stimulate himself to win the day, to triumph over the problem of the moment, or to beat the other guy. Turning obstacles into opportunities is another mark of a true leader. Walk with confidence and you will be a beacon whom people will follow.

Some people want to be leaders because they think that leadership is a kind of personality trait that will make them popular. They see confidence, the respect of others, kindness, self-containment and think that if they could just learn to be a leader, then they would magically have all of that. But that's not how it works. *Leaders are leaders because they are confident.* They are confident in themselves because they have already worked to overcome the obstacles in their lives.

*The foundation of confidence is trust.* When you trust yourself to have everything you need to succeed at what you put your mind to, then self-confidence radiates from you as a natural effect.

Because they have been through the hard times, leaders have natural compassion for others who are struggling to reach their goals. When you know how hard it is to be great at anything, you respect others for trying to get there.

**Because you respect them first, they will respect you.**

## Willpower: Maintaining That Fire

I owe my defensive prowess to sheer, stubborn will. I made myself a better defensive player in college because I saw the need to grow as a player and to develop some assets to distinguish me from the pack. I improved to become an All-NBA defensive player because I had the drive to put in the necessary sweat, pain and study.

I learned top defensive techniques by playing the game and watching the game. Experience and work ethic are the two greatest teachers I've ever had. In time, I merged my fiery desire to improve with some newfound lessons about shutting down opponents. That combination seemed to give me some momentum, a progression to go from a decent defender to one of the league's elite. In short, I gave myself a chance to get better.

At the bedrock of willpower are two things: your character and your standards. You simply refuse to compromise what's important to you and refuse to let failure get a foothold. That's the mindset. But loss, of course, is inevitable.

Three times (in 1998-1999, 1999-2000, and 2002-2003) I ranked among the top twenty players in the NBA for steals per game. So, while that stubborn determination helped me blossom as a better NBA player, it was also a valuable commodity in the down times – while I was working through injuries, dealing with bad losses or getting over bad individual nights on the court. Willpower can help sustain your passion during the occasional, unavoidable dips in your life.

When our coaches devise the team's defensive game plan, I often draw the opponents' top offensive star – like Dwayne Wade of Miami, Ray Allen of Boston or Chris Paul of New Orleans. When I'm facing explosive talent like that, there are certain nights when I'm just not going to put a dent in their point production. It's a given. Sometimes you get beat.

With a robust willpower, however, you are more willing to stay the course, to keep your head up and continue believing in yourself. If you have that resolute underpinning, it's always there to tap. It's a reservoir of positive energy.

Again, you can build your willpower over time by:

- Learning how to talk yourself through challenges

- Making plans and strategies so you are prepared for unexpected problems when they arise

- Living life. Experience gives you the security to know you have the tools to overcome trouble.

- Remembering the larger reasons for your struggle, like why it is so important to meet this goal.

As I like to say, there are opportunities imbedded in the bad times. And when opportunity meets preparation – when you have done all the pre-work, the practice and the positive self-talk – you can plow through the obstacles like a bulldozer.

As a leader, I have tried to help other players prepare and get their minds around the bumps ahead. Using my accumulated knowledge, I have tried to forewarn teammates about the rigors of life in the NBA.

During my second year in Cleveland, I often preached to LeBron James how the pace, intensity and energy of the regular season paled to the playoffs. He had never been to the post season. Little by little, I tried to prepare him for what lay ahead."I'm telling you – you think its hard now, but when you get in the playoffs, it's going to be a different animal," I told LeBron. "It will be so much tougher. Teams will know your plays. Every possession will be more important." Even with his vast talent, LeBron needed a mentor to walk him through the future, to help him prepare.

Maurice Cheeks did the same thing for me when he was an assistant coach in Philadelphia. Based on my weaknesses as a player, he warned me how teams were going to play me defensively. "You're not that great a shooter, so they're going to force you to shoot, force you to be a scorer," Coach Cheeks told me. So I entered the games mentally primed to be aggressive on offense.

You know that old saying, *be ready, willing and able*? It's no surprise that "able" is the last word in that sentence. If you are ready and you are willing, those two traits can trump any shortcomings you have in ability. As my mentor and friend Bishop Eddie Long likes to point out about me, everything in my life is deliberate and planned. I'm always ready.

Bishop Long has said he sees that forethought most in how I raise my kids. I make sure to construct my schedule in a way that makes my family a priority so that when I am with them, they get my undivided attention. I'd like to think that my boys don't even realize how much I travel due to the amount of full focus I give them when we're together. I am in the moment.

That doesn't just happen. That is pure calendar management. I think that's the key to finding balance in your life – carving out time for all your pursuits.

At the root of all that calculation lies preparation. But if willpower is a learned quality that means one thing: it also can be taught. There are moments in games – especially on defense – when I feel like I am willing guys to find something extra within themselves.

Time after time, I've been in situations in which the clock was ticking toward zero, and our team down a bucket. We needed a defensive stop. I was able to individually force a missed shot, deflect a pass or make a steal. You can sense the team's intensity level soaring immediately after that. That infusion of energy then rolled forward to our offensive possession where one of our guys made an equally brilliant play to score.

What I'm saying is that there are times you can physically or emotionally encourage people to do more than they're capable of doing, to find strengths in themselves they didn't know they had, and to help them believe that they are about to make a big play.

Shawn Respert loves to describe how my laser-like intensity flared in crunch time at Michigan State and helped galvanize the entire squad. He was the team clown: easy going, joking in the huddle. I was the polar opposite, glaring at Shawn for being so casual when the game was about to be decided.

"Be quiet! Let's get ready to play!" I would yell, all business. That would snap the rest of the team back into the moment and fix their attention on the job at hand. Sometimes, that burst of willpower served as an emotional catalyst to inspire our team to close the gap on an opponent when all seemed lost, to make a big comeback. You can *will* people to be great. With the right push, people can break through their own understood limits.

It's almost like the tale of the mother who, after a car crash, found the superhuman strength to lift the vehicle off of her child. In more realistic terms, I think of Paul Pierce, the Boston Celtics star forward who heard his knee pop during Game One of the 2008 NBA Finals against Los Angeles. He immediately thought he had torn a ligament. But just minutes after he was carried from the court and wheeled into a hallway to check on the injury, Pierce returned to the court with a black elastic wrap on his leg. His Boston teammate, Kevin Garnett, saw Pierce limping back into the game, clenched his fist, and screamed "Yes!"

Pierce scored another eleven points after the injury – twenty-two points total in the game – and helped the Celtics beat the Lakers ninety-eight to eighty-eight. "I knew I needed to be out there for my team," Pierce said later. His willpower had defeated the knee pain. In another sense, though, Pierce did what was within his power to return and contribute. He didn't take over and dominate the game after the injury. He simply did what he could to help his team.

As much as some of us may have the inner fire to do more, you have to remember a simple truth: you can only do what is in your power. It reminds me of a story of about my father.

I'll never forget my dad's parting words of advice the day I left home for college. It is the best advice I have ever gotten: He said simply, "Son, work hard and keep your mouth shut."

People have often commented on my work ethic, but I know I would have never made it to college, let alone the NBA, without my father's example. Though that was the first time that my father had ever said it out loud to me, he had already taught me that lesson in a far more powerful way. He lived it. He was a daily example of working hard without resentment, without complaint. He never gave less than his best. Without ever having to come out and say it, he taught me that:

**There is only one way to fail –
that is simply by not doing everything in your power to succeed.**

That doesn't mean that you will succeed at everything you do but, to my father, failure meant living with the knowledge that he hadn't done everything possible within his power to succeed. After that, it was out of his hands. If he "failed" by the world's standards, he was still a happy man because he knew beyond a shadow of a doubt that he had done everything in his power. He never failed himself, and he is a happy man. He gave me that gift just by being himself and doing what came naturally to him. The key concept here is "in your power." We tend to think that we can force things to happen.

**We get into other people's business, into God's business, and out of the only thing that we have any control over whatsoever – *our business.***

If you want to live an unhappy, frustrated, unsatisfying life, then focus on all the things that you *can't* control and try to change them. It sounds ridiculous on paper – but isn't that what 95% of the people in this world spend their lives doing? We're out of our business, into someone else's business. Then we wonder why we don't reach our goals and why we aren't happier or more content.

The one thing that I can affect – the *only* thing that I *can* affect – is myself. This is one of the most lasting and valuable lessons I've learned in my life.

*I can only do all I can do.*
*And if I do all that I can, it is enough.*

Most people rely on the world to tell them when they have done enough. We look for acknowledgement, approval and recognition from other people. This is one of the most damaging things we can do to ourselves.

No one else could ever know when I have done my best. The only person who can know that is me. If I wait for outward signs of recognition that I have worked hard and they don't come, then I start to doubt myself. I allow other people the power to determine how I feel about myself. If I don't get the recognition that I am looking for then, over time, I will come to doubt myself, my abilities – even my effort.

Because of my father, no one can tell me that I didn't work hard enough. If I don't get what I want, I know that it isn't because of something I didn't do. It is because of circumstances outside of my control – and that I can accept. There is a tremendous peace in that knowledge. What's amazing is that I work myself harder than anyone else ever could or would. Without my father's example of an iron-clad work ethic, I would never have known how to push myself past my limits and keep working – no matter what.

## Ball-You-Man

That's the mantra of good defense. In man-to-man defense, you're usually guarding a player without the ball. The proper technique is to always stay between the man you're covering and the player with the ball. You must constantly keep your eyes on both targets, moving as they move, maintaining that position between them. The idea is to cut off and prevent any pass between the two. In other words, you are multi-tasking.

A good leader doesn't think linearly. He thinks in 3-D. He looks at the whole process. NBA basketball games are not one-on-one affairs. I can't zone in on my defensive assignment and forget about the rest of the action. I have to watch the entire flow of the other team's offense, anticipating where the ball is headed next, preventing it from reaching my guy, or helping out if a teammate gets beaten to the basket.

How often in the workplace do you have the luxury of focusing on and completing one task at a time? Not often. It's usually a juggling act. The trick is to have the vision and concentration to balance those responsibilities equally.

That's a rare aspect of leadership and something most leaders don't have. They're either about guarding the basketball or focusing on their court position – but not both. Leaders must be able to weigh two, three or four items at once, to analyze on their feet, to study a variety of horizons simultaneously. They must press their fingers to the pulse of the present, yet keep their ears on what's coming next to be aware of all options on all levels. You know that old maxim: keep your eye on the ball. There's wisdom in that. At the same time, you'd better be aware of what the other players are up to. Leadership requires a broader perception – a three hundred sixty-degree vision plus the ability to truly hear your teammates.

One final facet of great defense is communication – a crisp exchange of information between five players. You have to hear where they are, what they need. You have to direct them. If I'm guarding the dribbler and one of his teammates sets a pick for him, one of my guys has a duty to shout that out to me as a warning – "Screen on your right!" This way, I don't get blindsided when I try to move laterally with the ball handler.

If one of my teammates gets beaten off the dribble along the baseline and his guy has a clear path to the rim, he's expected to scream "Help!" so that I can leave my man and instantly shift my attention to the more urgent priority – stopping his guy from dunking.

If you listen to a good defensive basketball team, you'll hear a chorus of chatter as they succinctly convey their positions on the court, their needs, what they see happening and what they think is coming:

"Switch!

"Heads up on the three!"

"I've got your help on your left side!"

"Force him left!"

"Force him right!"

If we're playing the Celtics, and Ray Allen is in the left corner, Paul Pierce is in the right corner and Rajon Rondo is at the top of the key, you can bet I'll be yelling to my guys to pressure Allen and Pierce so that Rondo ends up taking the shot (an offensive position I'm quite familiar with). Rondo is a great player, but the other two Celtics stars shoot for higher percentages.

Effective communication is crucial because it puts everyone on the same page to succeed. It's no different on the basketball court or in the boardroom: without talking to each other, people can go astray, take the wrong directions or waste time and energy because you're leaving it up to the individual to make his own way. There is no coordination or cohesion without clear communication.

This was once a weakness for me, but I forced myself to learn to be a better communicator at Michigan State. Actually, it might be more accurate to say that then Associate Head Coach Tom Izzo forced me to learn to be a better communicator. He demanded it.

I had always been more of a show-you-by-example guy. Under Coach Izzo, however, I become a guy who talked to his teammates. In time, I became more comfortable in that role. In other words, I wasn't born with a wide array of leadership skills, but I learned that there are no shortcuts to being a great leader. You have to put in the blood, sweat and tears to earn the right to lead, to have the ability to respect the people that you are leading and to have them respect you in return.

In a time when we idolize celebrities and are taught by constant media reinforcement that there is something missing inside us, understanding that leadership is an ability inherent to each and every human being is not just refreshing – it is absolutely *critical* to our future.

The misconception that some people are just born "special" to lead – or that leadership is a special talent granted only to a few – makes us not only willing, *but eager* to discharge our own personal responsibility to lead. At a time when the world is crying out for leadership, guidance and wisdom, the people most qualified to provide them are waiting for others to stand up. That, my friends, is just wrong. Leadership is not some *mysterious* trait. Every man, woman and child has the seeds of great leadership within him or her. It is no longer a luxury to develop that leadership – it is a *responsibility* that you have to yourself and to every person you come in contact with in your life.

You might think that some people are just "natural leaders."

**Leadership, while inherent in each of us,
cannot fully develop without unshakeable self-confidence.**

The people you might consider natural leaders are, in my experience, simply men and women who were either born or encouraged to develop the personality traits we admire in this society – an outgoing attitude, a driven spirit and a curious nature. The feedback they received as children was more positive than that of a child who might have been introverted, quiet or soft-spoken. The child who received more positive feedback from his or her environment naturally developed into a stronger, more self-confident person who then developed the leadership traits that are inherent in each of us. This is true also for any child fortunate enough to grow up with a strong, positive, encouraging influence. As long as the child is being encouraged and is growing in self-confidence, his or her natural leadership abilities will emerge.

Leadership is in no way about being extroverted or introverted. I have known great leaders who fall into both categories. I've been mentored by great leaders who never have to say much at all, but who have followers willing to walk through fire for them. They are able to inspire and encourage their people to reach and achieve their biggest dreams. I have also had the privilege to work with leaders who are very outgoing, social and talkative. These men and women are just as encouraging, just as inspirational – and they inspire just as much loyalty and gratitude in their people.

Now, I was certainly nobody's idea of a leader growing up.

**No one ever looked at me and said,**
**"Wow, that kid is just a natural leader."**

What I *did* have was the most amazing group of mentors and leaders who believed in me … nonstop. The greatest of my mentors was – and will always be – my mother, who relentlessly spoiled me. I was the youngest of seven siblings by almost five years – the baby. In my mother's eyes, I could do no wrong. No matter what I did, my mother was always on my side.

It is quite possible that without my siblings keeping me in line, and my father's guidance, I could have ended up a brat. But my mother's absolutely selfless, unconditional love made it safe for me to dream big. I write about this to emphasize one point: No one is a self-made man. Ask any rags-to-riches success story and he will tell you that it took a small army of people to get him where he is today.

It isn't just about having your own *personal* vision – although without it you certainly aren't going to get anywhere. It's about creating a reality in your life where your vision is important, believable and upheld by the people around you.

My mother is my biggest fan. That seems cliché because a lot of people are fortunate enough to be able to say that – but not everyone is. Now, I can't carry a tune in a bucket, but I've got a mother who, if I had said to her, "Mom, I'm going to be the next Brian McKnight," she would have replied, "I know you can do it, Pookie." (That's right. I said Pookie.)

She wouldn't have said it just because she thought it was the right thing to say or that she should say it. She would have believed it with all her heart and soul. I could feel it when she looked at me with that light shining out of her eyes like there was nothing I couldn't do. You have to have people like this in your life to become a great leader. If it's your mom, that's amazing. If not, then seek out people who believe in you and your dreams and completely surround yourself with them. If my mother gave me my dreams, then my father – a man of very few words – taught me everything I needed to know to make that dream a reality.

I guess that's how I did it. That's the real answer to the question at the beginning of the book. I was born into an environment full of love, support and expectation. Then I surrounded myself with people who cared enough to be honest with me. They held me over the fire until I was refined into the man I am today. They grew me up. They made me a leader. For that, I thank them all.

# Part 3:

# Creating High-Performing Teams

# Chapter 9:

# Sharing Your Vision with Your Team

### For Clearer Results, We Need to Share a Clear Vision

I cannot stress how important it is for leaders of high performers to create a shared vision and share that vision with the team. In business, just like in basketball, most of the problems that we face in leading high performers are simply due to the failure of the leader to show team members how they fit into the bigger picture. To do this effectively, a leader has to be able to motivate others. Not the "flash-in-the-pan," hyped-up, professional speaker motivation. It's a genuine, soul-stirring motivation. By looking at what actually motivates a person, an effective leader propels team members to work harder. When there is a clear vision, the team can turn on a dime and react to changes in the game plan or in the marketplace quickly and effectively. Not only do the players know *what* they need to do and *why* they need to do it, they also know that they are *capable* of doing what needs to be done. At this point, the coach can sit back and allow the players to do what they do best! The team players think and act like coaches. They have been given all of the information they need to make split second decisions, and they are motivated to give 100% all the time.

My first pro team, the Seattle SuperSonics, personified this polished approach. When I joined them as a rookie in the 1995-1996 season, the roster included veterans Gary Payton, Shawn Kemp, Nate McMillan, Sam Perkins, Detlef Schrempf and Hersey Hawkins. We won sixty-four games that season and went to the NBA Finals. Those notable players were all teachers in their own way, always willing to help a young guy learn about life in the league or about playing the game hard and right. They'd been through it all –including a devastating loss in the playoffs two years earlier to the Denver Nuggets. They could make decisions on the fly. It was ideal on-the-job training.

You see, in order for players to begin to act like coaches, or for team members to act like executives or company owners, leaders must take the time to educate each person about the vision and the value of following through. Personal responsibility and ownership of the vision is what turns a group of people with their own agendas and goals into a functioning unit capable of more than they are on their own. Creating a high-performing team requires the ability to establish a compelling vision and then impart that vision to the people in a way that causes them to get behind it. All people need is a common goal to move from being a group of individuals to being a team who can be successful in *any* endeavor.

This ability to create a shared vision is key to being a successful leader. It is critical and non-negotiable. My mentors and leaders all had a vision for their teams in addition to a vision for the individual players involved. Their vision allowed the players to come together, work together, bond, leapfrog off each other's strengths, and shore up one another's weaknesses. That's because the leaders and team players all spoke a common language based on a shared vision. Anyone can sort names into groups. Having a roster of names doesn't mean you have a team. Players who know what the vision is and can see how it benefits the group *and* themselves make a team.

Another reason vision is so critical to the success of the group is that it allows team members to monitor their actions without needing, and coming to resent, constant "parenting" from coaches. No one appreciates someone breathing down their neck and telling them what to do. A person's confidence is increased when they feel competent enough to carry out their particular goals and help the team move towards success. That confidence in individual members is critical to the success of the group – and is also the responsibility of the leader to create. The way this is done, again, is simply through creating a clear and shared vision and letting each player know where they fit into the bigger picture. Without it, team members operate under their own understanding of the vision as they see it. That could be a lot of different versions of the same vision, right? Some players could even be in opposition to another player's vision. This would create a situation ripe for conflict which only takes valuable time and resources away from where they are best used – moving toward the common goal.

Let's say, for example, that a coach neglects to create a shared vision with his players. During the season, a particular new rookie's vision might be to get at least twenty minutes of playing time per game. Now, you might think that this would be a good thing for the team. It could motivate the rookie to work harder and be a better player so he'd be worthy of that game time. But what if the team's vision is to win their conference? Let's say the team is going up against another team where the lineup is best served without the rookie ever setting a foot on the court – not because the rookie isn't talented or skilled, but simply because a different player has a style that is better suited to win against this particular team.

In the first case where the rookie has a vision only for himself, two things could happen: The rookie could do everything in his power to play in that game. He might even get some floor time, but he would be focused on his playing time and not necessarily on what is best for the team. This, frankly, is natural.

If a shared vision isn't communicated that encourages the players to understand that what is best for the team is also best for everyone individually, then individual players are will feel they are left to fend for themselves. This scenario can only create division within the team. There is a flow to a game when all of the players are working together and are committed to each other and to the plays. There is a very different flow, or lack of a flow, when players are out on the court with an "individual" mentality.

This can happen often with superstar performers. In business or in professional sports, when a superstar joins the team, it is critical to channel that powerful force into boosting the entire team; otherwise, the team could become the background for the star. This isn't good for anyone – not the team, not the star, not the coach, not the fans, not the game. First of all, it creates unnecessary pressure on the star to perform. This can lead the superstar to burnout and resentment. Secondly, it creates conflict within the team as the players feel less and less important. This undermines their self-confidence and that will show up on the court. Then, the star feels increased pressure. It becomes a viscous cycle that fosters competitiveness and animosity exactly where you absolutely don't want it – within the team itself.

It also creates a dependence on the star to carry the game. This is great when the star is having a string of great games. But what happens when the player has an off day, or worse, gets injured? If the team is used to depending entirely on this a player, it will fall apart when he isn't performing well or leaves the team. This is not the best way to run a team or a business. However if the team is operating based on a strong vision with shared values, individuals can come and go and the team will be little affected.

You can apply this need for a vision outside of the boardroom as well. Take families, for instance. You might be thinking that families don't have visions or goals. But they do. The families that operate most smoothly with the least amount of conflict and that create the tightest bonds are the ones that have very clear ideas about who the family is, what they stand for and in what they believe. It seems strange to speak like this about something as natural as family, but you can learn a great deal about building strong teams by looking at strong families. This doesn't mean that families should have a rigid vision for who their children should become. They shouldn't say: "In this family, we are all lawyers. In order to fit in and be accepted, you also must be a lawyer." Do you know families like this? It is damaging when the values and vision are not discussed, but merely implied. That way, if one of the family members doesn't fit into the system, he or she feels left out and may spend a lifetime trying to measure up to this unclear standard. This undermines self-esteem and creates conflict. Often, when a child feels left out of a family dynamic, it is because they aren't shown how they fit into the bigger picture.

And this is exactly what happens in most teams when a clear vision is not shared by the leader.

The happiest families – the ones with children who have high self-confidence and parents who have a loving, honest relationship – are, in my opinion, like the best basketball teams or the most successful business groups. They have a vision that everyone can get behind – one that is specific enough to motivate the players but broad enough to encompass everyone's talents.

In my family, we have certain rules and standards of behavior. More importantly, we have common values. The way we judge success is a perfect example of creating a shared vision that doesn't leave anyone out. For any success we experience, we answer these three questions:

1. **Did you thank God?**
2. **Did you try your hardest?**
3. **Did you have fun?**

It's like a secret language that my boys, my wife and I share. It creates a close-knit bond between us. My boys will ask each other these questions if one of them is having a down day. I notice that my kids get very frustrated when life doesn't go their way. They get visibly upset because they want to win and do well so badly. That's when we ask each other these three questions. We ask them daily and as a result, we function better as a family.

At some point, a common language around values and vision starts to develop and become unique to the team. Just as my family's 'secret language' allows us to come together, this common language begins to help the team better function as a unit – not as individuals looking for individual glory. On the teams that I have captained, we would invariably create this kind of language based on shared vision and values. It is a mark of a group that has moved from the individual ego to the collective ego.

And it is the mark of a leader who has learned how to use a shared vison to successfully lead high performers.

## Fast, Fluid and Flexible –
## On the Court and In the Boardroom

This is the type of leadership that is needed in today's fast-paced environment. There simply isn't time to train each new member on the team aboutevery aspect of the business. We need fluid, fast, and flexible strategies on the court and in the boardroom. This flexibility is seen in players who are allowed to be individuals because they are all operating under the overarching vision. Each player is valuable and thought worthy to be on the team or he or she wouldn't have been hired. They all bring their unique talents and strenghts to the team, and should be able to use them. By tapping into the vision, each team member is free to contribute to moving the team closer to the goal. In this manner, you get the full potential of every person on your team. Their skills, intelligence and energy are used to help push the vision through.

Contrast this with a team that lacks a solid, compelling vision. Now you have talented, intelligent people that are left to create their own vision that may have absolutely nothing to do with the overall goals of the organization. This is a waste of time, resources and the energy of your team members. It's no wonder that many teams in sports or business don't succeed. Without a common vision, people are looking in fifty different directions that pull them apart instead of push them together. Players on championship teams, whether in sports or business, are driven by a shared mission that transcends individual recognition.

An effective leader creates and imparts a vision that unites each member of the team and helps them focus on common goals. Vison brings the players together emotionally and also becomes a marker that directs each player's daily actions and decision-making. This leads to a sense of collective responsibility and pride, but also rewards players individually. Each player is motivated to work harder when he or she clearly understand his or her role and contribution to helping the team manifest that vision.

The ability to create an overarching vison and encourage team members to support that vision while showcasing their individual talents is what every leader strives to do. It is the difference between an average team and one that gets the championship ring.

And what leader doesn't want the championship ring?

---

### Thoughts on Leadership by Tom Izzo, Head Coach at Michigan State

**What are the top three qualities of a good leader?**

A leader must be able to self-evaluate and be critical when needed, knowing that they might not have anyone pushing them to get better. Without continual self-evaluation and motivation, a leader could become stagnant. A leader must instill confidence in those who follow, but first, they must believe in themselves. A large part of this comes from setting realistic goals that everyone buys into and truly believes can be achieved. A leader can only be as effective as those who are following. A leader must motivate and find a way to make everyone else better. This can be done by effectively communicating every step of a plan. An idea is only as good as a leader's ability to communicate it to others.

**What are the top three faults of a bad leader?**

People can see right through a phony person or idea. Then there are leaders who talk it, but don't walk it. If a leader is not willing to do something, how can they expect someone else to do it? But, regardless of how brilliant a leader might be, if they can't get anyone to believe in and follow them, nothing will come from their ideas.

**Who are the three most important leaders in your life and why?**

I have to begin with my father. He taught me life lessons of humility and the importance of a strong work ethic. As a group, my high school coaches had a profound effect during my formative years. They taught me the importance of excelling academically, athletically and socially. Later, when I was a young coach, Jud Heathcote taught me that everyone (whether it is a coach, a player, the media, the athletic director, or the school president) has a job to do and that we all have to answer to somebody. This understanding allowed him to communicate better with different people. Growing up, I also tried to learn as much as I could about Vince Lombardi from afar, but I didn't have a personal relationship with him. I thought he was a great leader, especially his ability to make everything seem so simplistic, yet remain so effective.

**Who are the three top leaders in NBA history and why?**

That's easy for me to answer: Magic Johnson, Larry Bird and Michael Jordan. All three of these guys personified great leadership. They won at the highest level, they constantly worked on their games, they always believed they were going to win, and they made their teammates better.

**Who are the three top leaders in the game today and why?**

Mike Krzyzewski has done the best job of maintaining excellence over an extended period of time. His teams have achieved, athletically academically and socially. Tubby Smith has shown the ability to handle tough situations with class and dignity, and through it all he continues to do so much for the game. He is respected by his peers for his actions on and off the court. Jerry Colangelo has given his life to the game of basketball. In his work with the USA Basketball Senior National Team, he saw something that needed improvement and was willing to think outside the box to find an innovative solution. I also admire the way he's been willing to hold people accountable, including some of the top players in the game today.

**Who are the three top leaders in the world today and why?**

These are three people who can teach us all something different. Bill Gates – Not only did he start Microsoft and build it into one of the most successful American companies; he's taken his enormous wealth and become one of the world's great philanthropists. He uses his status and wealth in an effort to make this world better, including inspiring others to take part in charitable activities. Earvin "Magic" Johnson – As mentioned earlier, Magic is one of the game's all-time greats, but it's what he's done since leaving basketball that makes him special. He's used his celebrity status to educate people worldwide about HIV/AIDS. He's become a successful entrepreneur, and continues to put resources into inner-city development in urban areas throughout our country. American soldiers – I was fortunate enough to visit the American troops in Kuwait twice over the last few years. It was certainly a life-changing experience for me. We could all learn lessons of sacrifice, unity and the strength of a common purpose from these brave men and women.

- 131 -

# Chapter 10:

# Leading Constructively

*"When a team outgrows individual performance and learns team confidence, excellence becomes a reality."*

~Coach Joe Paterno

I t wasn't until college that I really learned about leadership. As much as I wanted to play in the NBA, wanting it was not enough. Even working hard wasn't enough. And it was the same at Michigan State. I was the star player in my high school. But when I got to Michigan State, everyone was the star player from his high school. I went from being the star to being average – overnight. It was terrible, and it was the best thing that ever happened to me. Why? Because I had coaches that saw more in me than I saw in myself. This was when I began to learn the lessons of leadership.

I'll never forget that first meeting at Michigan State. I knew I was on time. I am certain that I was on time. The meeting started at 3 p.m., and I was there at 3 p.m. I got the biggest tongue lashing of my career. I was a freshman on the team, and I didn't know that being on time was not good enough. I should have been there twenty minutes early. Twenty minutes early was on time. I was twenty minutes late. This earned me a scolding from Coach Izzo, and I learned a few things from that experience.

First of all, Coach Tom Izzo was right. That wasn't the easiest pill to swallow for a cocky eighteen-year-old who was accustomed to being the star. Here's the important part: I was taken aback and a little upset, but I was not resentful of the scolding. I knew that Coach Izzo had no agenda other than making me the best player I could be and making the team the best we could be. Even as a kid, I could tell that his agenda was my agenda. His agenda was me – and every other committed player on his team. He wasn't trying to hurt me or break me down. He was just giving me the guidance that I needed to reach my goals. So I listened, and I followed his advice. That is the mark of a leader.

A true leader gives feedback to players, to family, to the sales team, to the Sunday school class, whomever. Their words, both positve and negative, come across as *feedback* – not as criticism or judgment. You can immediately spot someone who is unqualified to lead. His own agenda gets in the way. That person's "feedback" will cause resentment and unrest in the group every time. A leader without a personal agenda can give the same feedback, even use the same words, and inspire loyalty and determination in his team.

This is another reason why just attending a seminar on leadership or getting hired for a leadership position will not magically transform someone into a great leader. If you can't drop your agenda, no one will follow you. That's one of the first leadership lessons I learned from Coach Izzo. Simply stated: Get over yourself!

Coach Jud Heathcote, also at Michigan State, provided me with my next defining moment in my leadership education. I call this moment the "big one", and you'll see why. We lost a key game against Iowa during my sophomore season or, as I used to describe it, I lost the game. My team had been leading all game. As the game entered its final minutes, Iowa's coaches decided to exploit one of Michigan State's weaknesses: my free-throw shooting. The Iowa players were told to repeatedly foul me to put me on the free-throw line. As I missed the foul shots, they grabbed the rebounds and were able to chip away at our lead.

Now, my struggles at the free-throw line were already a bad memory for me. During my final high school game, we were up by a single point *and* had the ball. The other team, Jackson High, fouled me as time was running down. With the clock stopped and the gym pulsing with noise, I stepped to the line to try and give my team a three-point lead. I missed the first shot. Then, I missed the second one. Jackson High's players grabbed the rebound, raced down the court and scored as the buzzer went off. Game over. High-school career done. A failure to ponder for a long time.

Now two years later against Iowa, I faced another pressure-packed moments at the free-throw line. The opponents were sending me there on purpose. They were intentionally fouling me. It was their strategy. They were daring me to miss, and I missed. Iowa won the game. From that moment on, free throws became my personal nemesis. I went from being a star in my hometown to being a national joke. There I was left with little faith in myself and my shooting.

Soon after that Iowa game, I got a message that Coach Heathcote wanted to see me. That didn't mean that I was to call him at my convenience. It meant immediately, if not sooner. So, there I was, outside his office, and scared to death. I was scared he would take me off his starting line-up, put me on the bench because of my free-throw issue. Somehow, despite the sinking feeling in my chest, I worked up the courage to knock on the door. What happened in that office was possibly the most significant thing that would ever happen in my career.

Coach Heathcote sat me down and looked at me for a long moment. What he said shocked me. He said he didn't care about what the papers were saying. He believed in me. At a time when I'd lost almost all faith in myself, here was my college coach telling me that he believed in me. Not only did he believe in me, he said he believed that I had what it took to make it to the NBA!

You could have scraped my jaw up off the floor. I was a national joke. He was receiving all kinds of criticism from fans for keeping me in his starting lineup, and he sat me down and explained why he believed in me and what I had to offer. I walked out of that office dazed and elated. I don't know that I ever told him what it meant to me that day in his office … until now. (Thanks, Coach.)

From that moment on, I attacked basketball with a renewed fervor. I ignored every newspaper article, every joke, every internal doubt, and I refocused my effort. I had a new focus now. Coach Heathcote had laid out a plan for me to develop a skill and a gift that I could bring to the NBA.

## Being a Straight Shooter

The first thing I remember Coach Heathcote saying to the team is, "You'll hate me now and love me later." Coach Heathcote was willing to be unpopular with the team because he knew that giving us honest feedback was in our best interest and, therefore, in the team's best interest. I don't think any of us ever hated him. He pushed us and made us work harder than we thought we could, but we always knew he was doing it for us.

You'd be amazed at the number of "leaders" I have encountered in my life that are not willing to be unpopular with the people they are supposed to be leading. From teachers, to vice presidents of major corporations, to coaches and church leaders, there are a lot of people who just don't have enough self-confidence to handle even the *possibility* of being rejected. They are too scared to tell the honest truth to people who need to hear it in order to get where they desperately want to go.

There's a great line in the movie, *A Few Good Men*, in which Jack Nicholson's character exclaims, "You can't handle the truth!" A better statement would have been that Nicholson's character couldn't handle telling the truth.

The most effective leaders I have ever been privileged to know, work with or be mentored by are the ones that cared so much about helping me that they were willing to sacrifice the natural, human desire to be liked. That is true caring. If you really care about someone and you see them making choices that might hurt their chances of achieving a dream, aren't you naturally moved to say something to them, even if it will possibly make them angry with you in the moment? Whether or not you actually say anything is about how strong your self-confidence is. It's also about how much you care about that person.

It's easy to ignore problems, to rationalize not taking the harder road ... for a little while. In the end, it works out badly for everyone involved. Great leaders are willing to take the hard road right away because they know that, in the long run, everyone will be better off because they did.

Now, please don't misunderstand me, I'm not in any way saying that to be an effective leader you should be confrontational or a busy body who's always up in everyone's business. You know the difference between giving constructive feedback and stirring up trouble.

**Leadership means always asking,
"What is the best way at this moment to move
this person or this group toward the goal?"**

The point is that you can't shy away from confrontation as a leader. You don't have to get red in the face and shout, but you *do* have to be willing to tell people what they might not want to hear. We could all count on Coach Heathcote to be honest. That honest, accurate feedback allowed us to tweak and improve our games and really celebrate our progress. Coach was generous with his feedback – positive and negative. It made us better players, and we respected him in the end for it.

## Becoming What You Choose to Be

After I walked out of Coach Heathcote's office that day, I was a new person. Up until then, I was what my environment and natural talents had determined I would be. After that moment, I became what I chose to be. Coach left it up to me. He let me know – over the course of about three minutes – that I needed to rise to the occasion. Years later, Heathcote told me that even though he believed I could make it to the NBA, he had no idea that I would be able to go from a national joke to a thirteen-year career NBA veteran.

Each of us is faced with a moment in life that forces us to make a choice to *give up* or *get up*. That day, with my Coach's help, I made the choice to rise up and get better. That moment pushed me toward become the leader I am. I had to do the hardest thing any human being can do: I had to face myself. I had to look at my flaws head-on without defending myself or making them seem less important than they were. I had to look at myself and understand fully and completely that the only person standing in my way – the only person that could ever stand in my way – was me. That is the hardest thing any of us have to do, yet all of us *can* do it. We are all given the gift of choice.

You can go through life minimizing your weaknesses or lashing out in defense, trying to justify the behavior that keeps you unhappy, unsuccessful and disempowered. Or you can take that moment and choose to rise up. Grit your teeth and grab whatever courage you can and charge ahead. Life is forward motion. Once you accept the challenge to face yourself, to become a leader of yourself and of your life, you are there. It takes years to develop the skills and habits that make a leader, but it only takes a moment to make that result inevitable.

## Igniting Their Inner Passion

Another quality of leadership that can't be taught is the ability to see the highest potential in the people that you lead – and to work with them to develop that one true gift, their one true passion. Great leaders understand that we all have many *talents*, but only one *gift*. Everyone is gifted in some unique way.

**All the great, inspirational men and women throughout history are simply people who've recognized and developed their gifts.**

We teach our children today that they have to be good at *everything*. In school, they have to do well in math, science, reading, sports, making friends and maybe a hobby or two. If a child isn't doing as well in one area, all efforts are concentrated on developing that skill, regardless of whether or not it is a gift of the child. I'm not saying that we shouldn't all work to improve the areas where we struggle. We should – but not with the purpose of being good at *everything*. That's what I learned that day in Coach Heathcote's office.

He identified my unique gift in basketball as the ability to be an "old-school point guard." I wasn't the best shooter, not the best guard, not the best passer, but Coach Heathcote identified what I could do best and encouraged me to focus on that. You've probably heard about old-school point guards: the ball handler, the quarterback, the maestro, the coach on the court, the conductor, the general. Old school point guards run the team's offense by controlling the ball and making sure it gets to the right people at the right time. It's based on the concept of passing first and shooting second. It's easy to draw the parallels between our lives and this basketball position, isn't it?

With that idea planted in me by Coach Heathcote, I had a whole new outlook on my career – and life in general. I worked just as hard at improving my free-throw shooting as I ever had, but the effort was coming from a very different place. Instead of feeling like I needed to fix my game, I now realized that I needed to improve my game so that I could be the best point guard that I could be. Instead of feeling like there was something wrong with me, I began to work from a place of knowing that my greatest strengths were in what I did best and what came most natural to me. I was a student of the game. I understood the game. I could instantly visualize what needed to happen in order to score, and that was my gift to take to the NBA.

It sounds contrary to the way we are taught to think, but my shooting started to improve almost immediately. I was happy again on the court. When you work on developing your gifts, there is a different attitude toward work. It is more positive and optimistic, and it feeds your self-confidence rather than eating away at it. That can't be anything but a good thing – for me, for you, for your children, for everyone.

From that point on, I *knew* I could make it to the NBA. My dream had become a plan. The moment of my greatest defeat (and my coach's generous leadership) made it all possible.

## Raising the Bar

Being a good sport means a lot more than shaking hands with the other team after a game. Being a good sport means coming from a place of humility and having a team-focused mentality. Sportsmanship is a very admirable quality. It shows dignity, honor and humility. It is the opposite of the foul-mouthed, arrogant and selfish players that the media loves to show in the fifteen-second clips on the news.

Frankly, there are a lot more sportsmanlike players in every sport than there are arrogant athletes. For the most part, you don't get to be great at something without suffering a lot of setbacks along the way. Great players, great successes, great leaders have all had their share of hard work and hard times. Sportsmanship is born from the compassion that experience will bring. Some of the younger players, or overnight business successes, will lack the experience necessary to be good sports. And it shows.

Sportsmanship is an essential characteristic of a great leader because it is the ability to be positive and encouraging to others. Like so many other positive traits, sportsmanship has its roots in self-confidence. Self-confident people make good sportsmen, who make great leaders.

If you are confident in your ability to take care of yourself, to reach your dreams and to keep your commitments, then you can afford to support other people and be gracious doing it.

If you are always fighting that nagging fear that you aren't good enough, or if you're constantly making excuses for yourself and you don't have faith in yourself, then you will lash out at other people. No one wants to be around a bad sport – in athletics or in life. We don't like people who blame other people for their own shortcomings. We don't like people who are arrogant in victory and angry in defeat. We don't like people who make it about themselves all of the time – and we won't follow them if they try to lead us.

We know that if people are about their own agenda – to the extent that it causes them to lash out – then no matter what they say, their own personal agenda will *always* be the most important issue on the table. We simply can't trust them to lead us.

On the flip side, when we meet people who are humble in victory and gracious in defeat, we trust them to be able to control their own egos and agendas in order to let someone else have the victory. That is what true leaders do. They embrace the goals of the people that they lead. Those goals become their personal agenda. Being a great sport is essential to the ability to lead. You must be able to celebrate the successes of others.

You must be able to trust yourself to do the best you can everyday in training so that when the outcome isn't in your favor, you don't feel that you lost. Someone else was better.

You can't lose if you know that you did everything in your power. That sure knowledge, built on a lifetime based on a strong work ethic and the self-confidence gained from keeping your word to yourself almost guarantees that you can never lose. Therefore, you are ready and willing to support, celebrate and encourage the victories of other people. When you can do that, you begin to have what it takes to effectively lead others to victories of their own.

## Tapping Into Their Purpose

When the team wins, the individual wins. Howerver, it doesn't work the other way around. In order to succeed, the entire group must pull together. There is no room for egos, private agendas or attitudes. That doesn't mean that everyone has to have the same level of skill.

Sometimes we don't know what our gifts are. In my case, I had no idea that I would make a good old-school point guard. Coach Heathcote at Michigan State saw that gift within me and worked with me to develop it. This is so valuable when you are setting out on a new goal. It sometimes takes seasoned veterans, leaders, or mentors to help you find the areas where your greatest potential lies. In the absence of leadership, you have to find it for yourself.

Too many times, people try to make their natural talents fit what they *think* they want them to be or what they think they *should* be. For example, in basketball, defensive players are not as well-known as the superstar shooters and scorers. Most young players dream of being Michael Jordans or Allen Iversons, but that may not be where their gifts are.

If I had held on to my high school position of forward, I would not have been in the NBA. I had to be willing to take an honest look at my skills and actively work to be the best at my natural gift. That is what earned me a now thirteen-year career in the NBA. We all have natural gifts – areas in which we are uniquely wired to excel. These are things that we can do better than anyone else; areas where, if we work to hone the skills, we are unstoppable. If you try to force your nature to be something that it is not, then you will not only miss out on your opportunity to use the gifts with which you were born. If you focus on the gift you wish you had rather than the one you have, you miss out on both.

As a leader, it is your job to know all of the "positions" that you must fill on your team. You must know how each position is different, what the specific requirements are for each one, and the skills and talents of each of your players. In this manner, you can help steer them towards the position that is best suited to their natural gifts.

When you set *everyone* up to win, the whole team becomes extraordinary. Allow them to do what they do best, and, at the same time, come in and do what you do best.

## The Art of Listening

The ability to *truly listen* – without interruption or losing attention – is an underrated skill. However it is critical to master this skill if you want to give constructive feedback to your team. Whether you are listening to your children, your wife, your parents, your boss or your teammates, your ability to listen will directly affect the quality of those relationships.

Being a good listener requires more than just the ability to keep your mouth shut until someone takes a breath. It requires a quiet mind and, again, the absence of your personal agenda.

If you want someone to like you, or if you want them to think that you are as smart as (or smarter than) they are, then you aren't really listening to what they have to say. You are waiting for them to pause to take a breath so you can dive in with the sentence that you have spent the past thirty seconds forming to prove that you know as much or more about the subject than they do.

You can't be a good listener if you are just listening in order to come up with some convincing arguments to get someone to come around to your way of thinking. You can't be a good listener if you're thinking about getting back to the game on TV. Listening takes a quiet mind. You must be able to come from the position of *wanting to hear* what the other person has to say rather than *wanting to be heard*.

Listening also requires a powerful shift in awareness and is a gift that is not truly taught or readily accepted in our culture. We are taught to get our voices heard at any cost. In order to really hear what another person has to say, not what you think they are going to say or what you are afraid they are going to say or what you are hoping that they are going to say, you have to be open to what you are actually hearing in that moment. You must be able to let go of your personal agendas and desires and be receptive to receiving the information the other person is presenting.

I believe that the skill of listening is so difficult for us to do that it actually takes daily practice. I practiced listening. I would force myself not to say a word during a conversation until the other person was completely finished talking.

Let me tell you something: when the other person was my wife and the conversation centered around me not taking out the trash cans on time, this was not easy to do. But I discovered something miraculous. If I didn't interrupt her (or try to defend myself or try to calm her down) but truly just heard her out, all the fight drained from the situation. I genuinely heard everything she had to say. I thanked her for sharing herself with me and then, if it was still necessary, I would say my piece to her. I found was that most of the time it wasn't even necessary. We would be on to the kissing and making up part without ever having an argument.

Now, please don't misunderstand me and think that I am saying that you should stuff your feelings away or squelch what you feel you need to say. You absolutely should say it. Just be sure to listen as well as make your point. Honest, direct communication is the only way to create trust, friendships and real, lasting relationships in organizations and requires active listening from everyone.

---

### Thoughts on Leadership by Jud Heathcote, Former Coach at Michigan State University

**What are the top three qualities of a good leader?**
A good leader needs good communication, the ability to lead by example and the ability to command respect.

**What are the top three faults of a bad leader?**
A bad leader sets himself above others. He has poor communication, especially to people under him. He has no use for the people below him.

**Who are or were the three most important leaders in your life and why?**
Stener Kvinsland, my football and basketball coach in high school, made a lasting impact on me. So did Jack Friel, my college basketball coach at Washington State. Marv Harshman was my mentor in college basketball; I was his assistant at Washington State for seven years. I learned a lot from him.

**In your opinion, who were the three top leaders in the history of basketball and why do you feel that way?**

Magic Johnson approached the game as if winning was the only bottom line there is, and everything else related to that. Even though he loved the publicity, winning or losing was most important to him. Anytime a six foot, one inch or six foot, two inch player like Steve Nash can be the MVP of the NBA two years in a row, he has to have tremendous leadership qualities. Then there's Eric Snow, just for the way he worked and his approach to the game, his striving for improvement.

**In your opinion, who are the top three leaders in the league today?**

Steve Nash, Jason Kidd and Chris Paul are tops.

**In your opinion, who are the top three leaders in the world today and why do you feel that way?**

The head of China would have to be the No. 1 leader now just because of numbers. Yet, if you look at his approach to human rights, you would have to cross him off. It is almost sacrilege to say that Bin Laden might be the biggest leader in our world today and yet he's on our hit list for $50 million. Leadership as we know it is not the same as the leadership that others know. If you're looking at the United States at the present time Obama and McCain are great leaders because of the issues they had to face during their candidacies.

# Chapter 11:

# Managing Conflict

*"First keep the peace within yourself, then you*
*can also bring peace to others."*

~ Thomas à Kempis

People who lack self-confidence are highly defensive. They spend a lot of time and energy projecting a persona that mimics the way they want to be seen because they don't really believe in themselves. When that persona experiences criticism or feedback, the person becomes sensitive because their entire image is built on nothing real or substantial. If you are more concerned with how otherssee you rather than in how you see yourself, their criticism and disapproval can affect you very badly.

This way of thinking makes people defensive and it is very difficult for them to receive feedback that could be very helpful. Instead, they are likely to engage in conflict with the very person who wants to help them. This is a common issue in the world of sports. When a person is open to feedback and can handle contructive criticism without seeing a challenge or reason to engage in conflict, that person is coachable. Coachability exists in a variety of degrees in players and is absolutely necesssary for long-term growth and success in any area of life. A player who is coachable is one who is confident enough to know that he doesn't know everything. He trusts himself to learn, grow and become better. He actively seeks out advice and feedback from people that he respects, and he follows up on that advice.

So what are some other reasons people in sports and in business might find themselves in conflict with one another? For starters, they may have different views about the goal or vision they are striving for. They could have a different set of values, beliefs and opinions. Rapid changes also lead to conflict as individuals' responses to that change can range from approval to fear of the unknown. Finally, we find ourselves in conflict with others simply because we lack the sensitivity to different levels of ability, and our expectations for what others can achieve may be far off the mark from what they in fact can deliver.

Now imagine if you are leading a team of people and trying to keep them focused on your vision. Conflict arises as it surely will when you are leading high performers who feel that they are capable people with an opinion, and a right to be heard and respected. And this is natural. We all feel that we are experts about one thing or another, and it can be difficult to hear a different opionion about an issue or problem when we feel strongly about our position and the way we see the situation. That said, there are ways to manage conflicts of this kind.

Some leaders tend to use a more authorative approach and simply decide on a solution to the issue without input from the disputing parties. Not the best tactic, in my opinion, especially when you are dealing with high performers who want to be heard. Another less than perfect tactic is avoidance. Here, leaders simply ignore the signs of conflict and hope that the issue will either go away on its own as opposed to dealing with the team members head on and seeking a resolution that will appeal to both parties.

The best way to deal with conflict, in my opinion, is find a collaborative approach that allows you to broker a compromise between all parties, whether the conflict is between you and someone you lead, or between two or more people you lead. Either way, this method has far more appeal and far reaching positive affects as it is based on finding win-win solutions that build the team up as opposed to tearing it down. Most importantly, your team members are watching and learning from you as you handle conflict in a way that is respectful and impactful.

## Managing Conflict: The Leadership Checklist

Over the years, I've learned a great deal about managing conflict, and I have prepared a Leadership Checklist that will help you reduce and manage – or even avoid – conflict within your group. These are my own personal methods and they have worked very well for me.

### 1. Communicate in direct, easy-to-understand language.

Don't use fancy language or big words to try and impress the people you lead. Speak clearly and simply. People appreciate your direct honesty far more than a long, dialogue. Trying to look smart or impressive will only turn off the people that you are trying to connect with. Think about your own life experiences for a minute.

### 2. Create a culture of trust that minimizes conflicts.

You must be able to create trust within your team. They have to know that they can trust you to keep your word and hold up your end of the bargain. You set the tone for the entire group.

If you keep your word and honor your commitments, your team members will do the same. This creates a natural culture of trust and respect, and then, by nature, reduces the conflicts that arise within a team or organization.

Companies spend millions of dollars hiring consultants to create positive, productive environments, but it really starts with the simplest and most basic agreements. Your team's culture is a direct reflection of who you are, and if you are a great leader, your team culture will be a supportive one with minimal conflict.

## 3. Become a learner and a doer.

Learn and improve procedures that relate to your goals. When Coach Heathcote first blew my mind by telling me that he believed I could make it to the NBA and started training me as an old-school point guard, I had no idea what a powerful impact it would have on my life.

I believe that single moment was responsible for my success in the NBA. It taught me that I needed to take the responsibility to understand and improve the play on the court – not just from my position, but from everyone's position. That mentality makes for great leadership.

I wasn't the best shooter in the NBA. I wasn't the best guard in the NBA. But I was able to take something that I did well and hone it into a skill that I didn't even understand the value of until much later. I believe every leader should adopt the mentality of an old-school point guard.

Knowing and understanding each team member's contributions and how they help reach the team's goal is so critical to being able to make the rapid-fire, split-second, high-pressure decisions that make the difference between a win and a loss – whether you're on the court or in the boardroom. If I truly understand what it takes to make a good *offensive* play, then I understand what the *defensive* players need to do to set up the best play possible. I minimize unncessary conflict when I use people in such as way where their talents are maximized and they feel they are really contributing to the team.

If I have my eyes open to all the positions and their separate and unique tasks and goals, then I can always come up with ways to innovate and improve plays. But, if I'm here to do just my job, then I am not looking to succeed as a team. I'm looking to succeed as an individual. I'm looking for an excuse when I fail. I want to be able to say, "It wasn't my fault. The point guard set up the wrong play. I was doing my job." Being an old-school point guard in every part of life means that you are always looking to get the whole job done – not just the job you are assigned.

Great teams in every walk of life do this. History-making, awe-inspiring endeavors are accomplished by a determined group of individuals who share this philosophy. They all actively look to improve the procedures that relate to the goals. They know just enough about what everyone else on the team is doing that they can be the most effective in their own position.

On any team I have ever captained, we all *expected* that kind of leadership from every man on the court. Of course, this requires a certain humility that doesn't come easily or naturally to everyone. It's something you have to work at – especially if you're a superstar who has excelled and been celebrated for his or her talents since you could walk. Or if you're a successful businessman or businesswoman who is convinced of your own superiority. This is where egoless leadership comes in.

## 4. Keep the big picture in mind.
Setbacks and defeat will happen. In terms of morale and maintaining a positive focus in the face of these setbacks, a great leader is always measuring attention to detail against the big picture and helps his team members do the same thing. Setbacks in business or defeats on the field can make the possibility for conflicts highly likely.

At times like these, a leader must be able to keep the team actively moving toward their goals. Sometimes setbacks can be devastating. Without minimizing the effects of these setbacks, making light of the event, or engaging in denial, leaders can look defeat fearlessly in the face when they are able to keep their focus on the big picture. Leaders must be able to understand the difference between losing a battle and losing the war. Doing so will motivate team players to accept responsibility for those moments that don't go so well without resorting to blaming others and the inevitable conflicts that follows such behavior.

In summary, let me also suggest to you that disagreements can have a positive side as well and don't neccesairly have to become intense conflicts. Disagreements can actually lead to positive discussions that can generate creativity, innovation, and can build trust within your team. When you create a culture that rewards honeslty and integriety, your team players are more likely to speak their minds in a respectful manner, and the results of such conversations can have a tremendous impact on your team and overall vision.

# Chapter 12:

# Peak Performance

*"How do you go from where you are to where you want to be? I
think you have to have an enthusiasm for life. You have to have
a dream, a goal, and you have to be willing to work for it."*

~ Jim Valvano

### There's No Such Thing as an Off-Season

From July of 1998 through January of 1999, the NBA shut itself
down. Players weren't allowed on the courts – not even to practice.
We weren't getting paid It was a difficult time. At the beginning, we
figured the lockout would last for a few weeks, at the most. The guys
were cool at first.

I was with the Philadelphia 76ers at the time. We worked out
wherever we could, waiting for the lockout to end. My friend Michael
Curry – then a player with the Milwaukee Bucks and former head
coach of the Detroit Pistons – found a church with a basketball court
in suburban Detroit (which is where we made our home at that time).
Well, it was sort of a basketball court. It had a tile floor, but at least it
was somewhere to work out.

We met there five days a week where we ran drills and played.. It
Was hard on the body – I hurt like I never had before – but it was the

only place where we could play whenever we wanted. At first, many guys came to the makeshift court to practice.

But, as the weeks dragged on and became months, fewer and fewer players showed up. The lockout was hitting a lot of players hard. We trained for hours each day, five days a week, for months without pay. It was tough to keep going to that church every day for our pick-up practices.

But my inner circle – from my cousin, to my brother, to Larry Brown – drilled it into my head that there was *no such thing as an off-season*. Eventually, the lockout would end, and when it did, I would be ready. And when it did, I was ready.

Because the lockout had taken so long to resolve, we only had a few months left to play. The owners decided that they would make it a fifty-game season – fifty games in ninety days. Talk about hard on your body! We were on a grueling schedule. Most of the time, we played five games a week and often played three consecutive days. However, I was ready. We were ready. Why? Because, to us, we weren't "off." We had practiced. We had gotten up and continued to be serious about being professional athletes. There is no off-season.

The Sixers made it to the NBA Playoffs that year – and the next – ending an eight-year absence from the post season. The year after that, we reached the NBA Finals. To this day, my buddies give me a hard time about my "no off-season" mentality. We'll go to play a pick-up game and they are all like, "Relax, man, we just wanna have some fun."

I am having fun, and I don't know how to do it differently. When I am playing ball, I am playing to win, to do my best, to get better, to play with an in-season approach so no bad habits will creep in. Ever.

## My First Professional Game a.k.a. Pride Goeth Before a Fall

Once I got into the NBA, I realized that my basketball (and life) education had just begun. It was just like any job someone gets just out of college. In my first NBA game, I received one of the biggest lessons of my career from former Utah Jazz and NBA Hall of Fame point guard, John Stockton. As a younger player emerging through the college ranks, I'd watched the 10-time NBA All-Star and U.S.Olympic Gold Medalist on TV plenty of times. I had always marveled at how the other players could never seem to contain or guard him well. He was so competitive and knowledgeable. It didn't take long to recognize that this was the guy in charge and who the other players looked in all important situations. He always seemed to get the best out of his teammates while at the same time demanding excellence from himself. That impressed me.He'd always given me hope that I really could make it in the NBA because he just didn't "look like" he could dominate. In that first game of my professional career, I found out why he was one of the best point guards to ever play in the NBA.

That day, I thought I could just push him around and use my athletic ability to pressure him and give him trouble defensively. Well, on my first action, I had to guard John, and instead of being disciplined and adhering to the game plan, I tried to play overly aggressive defense, thinking I would have the advantage over him. Before I even knew what happened there was a lay-up and easy basket for Stock. As a matter of fact, the Jazz went on a run. A timeout was called for the Sonics. It was back to the bench for this rookie. I got schooled that day for sure.

It taught me something incredibly valuable. Never *underestimate* someone else's abilities – and never *overestimate* your own. Everyone who is in the NBA is there for a reason, and everyone who is in your company, your family or your church is there for a reason as well.

NBA players are the best in the world. I learned to respect every player in the league. I realized that I had something to learn from each of them. Pretty soon, while I played with the SuperSonics, I was on the court with the Bulls and the Lakers. I played Shaq and Kobe and Michael Jordan.

I remember walking out onto the court for a game with the Bulls early on in my rookie year. I looked up, and there was Michael. On the court. With me. Playing ball. With me. That was the moment that it really sank in. I had made it to the NBA. All my dreams, all my hard work, all the sacrifices I'd made had been worth it. I had made it. But making it wasn't good enough. I wanted to play. And if I was going to play, I was going to have to get better.

## No Such Thing As Luck

A lot of people talk about getting a "lucky break" on their road to success. Many said that my 1998-1999 season was my lucky break. But here's the truth on that: throughout my entire life, I've gotten where I've gotten by being ready. You can ask anyone who knows me. My life's equation has always been:

### Preparation + Hard Work + Opportunity = Success

If I had given up when I didn't make my high school's starting lineup all those years ago, I would most likely be working in corporate America and not in the NBA. If I'd quit during the 1998 NBA lockout, I wouldn't have been ready for the months remaining in that season. My NBA teammates and I continued to work hard even though we weren't playing games or getting paid.

## Preparation Meets Opportunity

Being prepared is being *proactive*. Relying on talent or luck to see you through is *reactive*, and maybe not the smartest avenue to take. Talent will only take you so far. The rest is based on proactive, determined, consistent practice. No one gets to the top by being talented. You have to be talented *and* be willing to work harder than everyone else. If you take a shortcut to the top – in any endeavor – eventually your lack of training, preparedness and experience will catch up with you. Once it does, you won't have the mental stamina or the emotional resilience to handle the fall.

I was talented, but definitely not as talented as other players. I had to work that much harder and longer if I was going to make it. But the great news is that hard work and determination will *always* win out over talent if there's no solid work ethic.

Being *proactive* will always move you towards your goals. Being *reactive* is a crap shoot. You might react well, or you might not. Being *reactive* is staying up all night drinking and eating bad food because you were stressed the night before the playoff game.

Not taking the time to weigh the pros and cons of a situation or to sit with the decision and then take the best course of action is a way of reactively sabotaging yourself. Proaction keeps you *prepared* for success. It keeps you ready. Luck is simply *opportunity* meeting *preparedness*. This view of luck keeps you in a positive frame of mind, because, as you know, life is not always easy.

When I was traded from the Seattle SuperSonics to the Philadelphia 76ers, it was a bad time for me. But, practicing the proaction I'd learned in college and with the SuperSonics, I focused on all the positives of the situation. I was going to get to play. So, we packed up and headed out to a new town and a new team.

In 1998 there was a lottery pick, and they'd drafted a guard – Larry Hughes. He was to play alongside Allen Iverson. But, just like in high school, I planned to be ready. I would be prepared. I would be proactive. Little did I know, but I was part of Coach Larry Brown's master plan – as an old-school point guard – to partner with NBA all-time great, Allen Iverson. It was my chance of a lifetime. And I was ready.

That's why you must stay prepared. Your chance could be right around that next corner. Don't let your ego or pride get in the way.

## 6 Steps to Becoming a More Fluid Leader

The fluid leader knows that progress is made in inches, not miles. Not everybody can get a home run every time at bat; otherwise people would stop paying to see professional sports! Instead, we must focus on a variety of small, key factors that underscore what it means to be a truly fluid leader.

Particularly in these challenging times, leaders now more than ever need to focus on a series of small progressions that will payoff in bigger results down the line. High performers often don't understand this concept and want to score a 3-pointer every shot.

What happens when they don't? Frustration followed by failure. This makes the high performer's job a moot point, your job extremely difficult and everyone else on the team down and depressed. In short, it's no way to perform, let alone lead.

The fluid leader can follow my **6 P's of Leadership Potential** to ensure that every day is a good day, every step is a step forward, and that even failures become potential successes when high performers are handled in a way that just keeps them moving.

## The First P = Planning

Be prepared – and equipped – for all challenges and succeses that come with leading high achievers. High performers don't want to know how many outlines you've made, how many pieces of scratch paper you balled up and tossed away, how many spreadsheets you filled out or how many hours you spent on planning last week. Fact is, nobody does.

However, this type of constant, permeating and ever present planning is absolutely crucial to your success with high performers. You may think that being fluid is all about going with the flow and being able to adapt. And, it is. However, the more you plan for success, the more you know what it looks like in all stages – beginning, middle and end game.

You know your team's potential for success inside and out. When changes are forced upon you, when a key player doesn't show up, when sales are down or budgets get slashed, your careful planning for success allows you to respond quickly – and successfully.

## The Second P = Priorities

You absolutely have to prioritize to create a winning team environment. And I don't mean prioritize the high performers above everybody else! I mean prioritize what is important to you as a leader so that you can communicate that theme back to the team so they can then adopt it both personally and professionally.

Remember, whether it is your leadership style or not, all leaders "lead by example." Your team, your crew, your department, your charter, your organization intimately watch, record and remember everything you do, say or emote. If you hold something as important – your church, your family, your health, your favorite charity, your net worth – the team knows it.

So as a leader it is important to prioritize which values you wish to share with the team. You will want to immediately establish the value of positive character along with individual and team discipline in order to develop a positive group or team identity.

## The Third P = Progress

Progress is essential to success, and I am sure this isn't news to you. However, what may be news is that your team's progress is up to you. The call *for* progress, the drive *to* progress and the evaluation *of* progress – i.e. what defines "success" for you and your team – are all leader generated.

Of course your top performers must do what they're hired to do – **perform**. However, it is *your* job to insure they are performing at pace, in a forward motion and up to your demanding standards. What's more, they have to a.) know what those standards are and b.) know that there will be benchmarks along the way so that progress **can be measured**.

How will you measure them? There are several ways you can do this. You can compare the current quarter's sales results with those of last quarter's. You can test this year's productivity against last year's and/or have regular quotas you expect to be met. This is Management 101 stuff; what takes it to the next level – what helps you lead top performers – is insuring that progress happens in a way that is reasonable and measurable.

## The Fourth P = Perseverance

Perseverance is, hands down, one of the most critical factors in becoming a more fluid leader. In fact, the very definition of "fluid" contains the word "flow." In other words, fluid leaders don't stop; not for obstacles, for injuries, for recessions, for layoffs, for pink slips, for down quarters, for up quarters, for relocations or for earth, wind and fire!

To lead is to persevere; to be a fluid leader is to keep going even when those who say they are going to perservere stop. Remember: lead by example. You don't have to give your team the big, "Little Engine That Could" locker room speech every morning; you just need to keep going, keep pushing, keep fighting, keep evolving – keep fluid – when obstacles do arise.

Part of perseverance is something we call compromise; you can't get your version of perfection every day at the office. People will get sick, people will disappoint, people will stumble, people will fall, people – even top performers – will fail. Perseverance doesn't always look triumphant with flashing lights and sweat dripping as you score the final basket just before the buzzer sounds or cross the finish line two centimeters ahead of your enemy.

Sometimes perseverance simply looks like forward motion, even if you need slo-mo photography to see it. Most of the companies who will survive this recession and go on to flourish when the slow economy is just a bad memory will be those who are right now, at this very moment, inching forward, day by day, sale by sale, hire by hire, play by play.

They are not always the Apples revolutionizing the iPod or the Cokes introducing a new flavor or even the Trumps building a new building. They are often simply inching forward quietly under their own steam, assessing progress on a daily – versus a quarterly – scale.

## The Fifth P = Patience

Be mindful that success is coming, but you have to be patient. Looking for individual or personal improvement from high achievers may take time. This is what often frustrates those who lead high performers; they work on their own schedule and yet must work within a schedule set by you, by the board, by the team, by the economy.

But you don't hire top performers to be mediocre or play by the rules. What top performers do and do well often requires a deeper and greater understanding of their process. It can take time to think up great ideas, introduce new products, or find the right candidate.

You must be willing to invest the time it will take you to a.) find a top performer, b.) train a top performer and, most important of all, c.) nurture a top performer. It is often this "nurturing" process that spells the downfall of most leaders of high performers.

And, absolutely, you can't coddle or "baby" a top performer. You must be willing to be patient and wait for those flashes of geniuses, those master strokes, those absolutely stunning ideas that make them top performers in the first place.

## The Sixth P = Partnership

Partnership is key on any team, but particularly so when a.) top performers often feel "above" the team and b.) other team members often resent a top performer's "favored" status.

Early on it will be important for you to establish a culture that stresses that both the ndividual and team will be better if strong relationships are built.

This is not a luxury; team-building and relationships can't be seen as "soft skills" because partnership is absolutely vital to your team's success. Teams must work together to succeed and it is your responsibility to foster a team mentality by creating strong relationships. The beauty of relationships is that they are addictive; once you have a cohesive team they will not only work together but will want to work together.

## Flexibility – Playing All Positions

The flexible leader is prepared for everything; partly because he = is already Fast and Fluid but also because he knows how to play all the positions himself.

Leaders know every key position and are poised to play them when needed in order to be successful. When they **Play All Positions**, they can effectively lead high performers because they understand where they're coming from:

- **Communication** (This is your point guard position): Good leaders articulate the viewpoints of management to high performers in setting goals and themes for success. Equally important is the articulation of ideas, thoughts, and experiences of high performers to management for better working conditions and overall success.

- **Action** (Shooting guard position): Leaders recognize that consistency and results are important to high achievers. Therefore backing up rhetoric with action and being consistent in your dealings will be crucial. Leaders will have to score major points with the high performer to gain their respect and trust. They can best do this by practicing what they preach.

- **Balance** (Best all around position): Leaders need to have a visibly noticeable handle on mastering the basic elements of life (physical, emotional, mental/spiritual, and the social). Leaders have to show that they can multi-task well. Leaders will need to score or show the ability to score big in the eyes of the high performer. The ability to do this well often times result in the high performer seeking you out as their role model.

- **Anchor** (Center or foundation): Leaders can keep their team of high performers in check by showing strength in good and bad times. High performers respect leaders with strong opinions rooted deep in their character. Leaders must be strong and stick to their ideas to show that they cannot be easily swayed.

- **Dependable** (Power Forward position): Successful leaders are both innovative and reliable. They make it easy for their team to predict their beliefs or expectations on a variety of topics regarding success. Erasing doubt from your team through effective and efficient productivity helps convince high performers that you are the correct leader to help them become successful. Make sure both the high performer as well management knows what they are going to get from you.

## "Just Enough" Is Not Enough for Peak Performance

In between doing just enough to get by and being a perfectionist lays a lot of middle ground. But I can tell you this: In my life, *"just enough"* would never have been enough to get me into the NBA. As a leader, you have to know how to push yourself so you can help your team push farther and harder.

I know that's also true for whatever field you are working or growing in. No one can tell you what your maximum is. You can be working hard, but only you know if you are operating at your peak. The results you want will only come when you go above and beyond, putting forth more effort than you think you can give and pushing yourself day-in and day-out until doing more than you did yesterday becomes a way of life.

This isn't some crazy self-help mantra, and it's not meant to be an impossible goal.

This is simply a mentality that you want to develop – a mental approach to how you treat your work. Let's say that I run a certain trail everyday. Instead of setting out with the goal of just "getting it over with," I set out with the goal of improving my previous time. Perhaps I set an additional goal of adding some push-ups to my routine as I pass the local park to make it even more challenging. Basically, you want to push yourself a little further and a little harder in the direction of your dream every day.

## It isn't the actual activity that matters.
## It is the mindset *behind* the activity that matters.

The right mindset will make all the difference in the world for you. It just makes sense that if you discipline yourself to approach your training sessions with a forward-thinking mentality, you will constantly move forward, always getting stronger, better, and faster. But if you go to your training sessions with the mentality that you just want to get it over with as quickly as possible, then you are not only going to fail at getting better, but you will also lose your edge. Again, your ability to understand this concept will help you impart the importance of having the right mindset to your team.

I thought I had worked hard at basketball, but when I got into the NBA I realized that I had hardly scratched the surface of what it meant to work hard. I remember going running with Detlef Schrempf soon after joining the Seattle SuperSonics.. This man is six feet, nine inches tall, and he can run forever. He is a machine. Just by being himself, by demanding excellence from his own training sessions, he challenged me to do more, to work harder in my sessions.

Every great player, every success story will tell you the same thing. Talent is never enough. Being great takes working harder than everyone else – every single day. If you approach every day of your work life with a sense of drudgery and obligation, you will get poor results. Of course, if you are doing something that you just aren't cut out to do, you will feel the effects of that, too. It is important to find your passion, your unique gifts and work to develop them, because if you love what you do, it makes developing a superstar work ethic much easier.

You will set yourself up to succeed. However, if you don't have the "do-whatever-it-takes-to-succeed" attitude, you won't succeed – no matter how much you enjoy what you do. In my experience, leaders rise to the top in everything they do. I believe that if a leader with a natural talent for developing small businesses was suddenly placed in an entry level position at a tax accounting firm, that leader would soon rise to the top.

As I said earlier, when I joined the SuperSonics in 1995, they were one of the top teams in the NBA. We had an all-star lineup including Gary Payton, Shawn Kemp, Nate McMillan and Detlef Schrempf. My coach told me at the beginning of the season that he didn't believe rookies had any right to play in the NBA. I wanted to play, though, and I was willing to do anything to play. So I talked to my coach. He gave me some simple but very powerful advice. He took me off to the side and pointed at Gary Payton. He said, "Look, Eric. Gary brings it – every day, every time. You don't. If you want to play, watch Gary, and do what he does." So I did. I watched and I practiced. I trained harder than I ever had. It paid off. I received more playing time than most younger players received during that time from Coach Karl.

## You Are Who You Hang Around

If you have nine broke friends, you are bound to be the tenth. I learned early on that the people I hung around would influence who I would become in the NBA and in life. We all must apply this concept to our lives every single day. On the other hand, we also need to be the kind of people that others *want* to hang around to improve themselves. God blessed me my first few years in the League while I was with the SuperSonics. There were a number of players and leaders who I was fortunate enough to "hang around" and learn from.

For example: **Nate McMillan** showed me the kind of leader and professional player that I wanted to be. **Gary Payton** taught me about true grit. He went out there to win every time. He expected to win. He demanded that we win. **Sam Perkins** taught me to think like a professional. He taught me early on that there was a life *after* the NBA that I needed to prepare for. He stressed the importance of how I spoke and dressed, and the importance of my overall appearance. He taught me how to speak properly and express myself appropriately in interviews.

**Hersey Hawkins** taught me how to be a husband and father while pursuing my dream of professional basketball. **Detlef Schrempf** taught me how to work, prepare my game and condition for the NBA. He also showed me how to pursue business opportunities and network for post-career planning while playing.

Of course, I wasn't thinking of any of this – or even aware of what I was learning – at twenty-two years old. The only thing on my mind was getting to play. But in everything *they* did, in the way they were, these men molded the way I thought – often without needing to say a word. I am who I am today, with the career that I have had, because I was picked up by the Seattle SuperSonics and blessed to be part of such a great team.

### There Are No Neutral Players in Your Life

No one wants to be in the position that the misguided Emperor (in the children's fairytale *The Emperor and His New Clothes*) found himself in. Yet, so many celebrities and leaders end up there. They have fallen prey to "yes men." As a leader, I need to be surrounded by people who will tell me their honest opinion of a situation. If you are surrounded with people who tell you that every decision you make is a good one, that every play you choose is the perfect one, that every breath you take was better than the last, then you are headed for a very unhealthy place.

Leaders cannot afford to be surrounded by people who lack the self-esteem and personal security to speak the truth. In my world, both professionally and personally, I work hard to surround myself with people who challenge me and question me from a loving place. It will become important for you to create a mastermind team of people who are strong, independent and willing to give you honest, caring feedback.

It can take a lifetime to build a strong mastermind group, so don't get discouraged if you look around and discover that you have only one or two people – or sometimes, not a single person – who you are willing to align yourself with. Some of my mastermind partners are men that I have known since I was a child. Some are members of my church. You will build up a strong team as long as you keep away from the deadly trap of the yes men.

My strongest mastermind partner is, and has always been, my wife DeShawn. I am fortunate to have married a strong woman who isn't afraid to speak her mind, right from her heart. She will always give me her honest opinion.

Another very good friend, Monty Williams, has always been a part of my life and one of the most brutally honest people I know. I've always been thankful for him. Throughout my entire professional NBA career, I've heard folks say how good or bad Eric Snow, the basketball player, was. What has always made Monty different (and what I really appreciate about him) is that he is the one person who gave me constructive criticism and also challenged my faith, heart, soul and mind. He once wrote me a heartfelt letter that, to this very day, has been a constant reminder to me to stay humble, thankful and giving with love. With all the distractions that can come while playing pro ball, he was able to capture my attention in a way that affected the rest of my life by helping me keep things in the proper perspective. Monty is indeed God's vessel sent to me. This type of support from a teammate was unbelievable. He was a leader stepping out in faith to help someone who, at times, thought he had all the answers. The best part is I still get all of this and more from our continued friendship to this day. Thanks, Monty, for being you.

## Thoughts on Leadership by Allen Iverson, Memphis Grizzlies

**What are the top three qualities of a good leader?**
He leads by example. He also tries to do everything the right way. A good leader plays the way the coach wants it done.

**What are the top three faults of a bad leader?**
Being an individual instead of playing for the team, going half speed, not giving everything you've got and failing to play the way the coach wants make you a bad leader.

**Who are or were the three most important leaders in your life and why?**
Of course I believe my mom, Ann Iverson, is a great leader. I am proud of the way he's represented me, so I'll also say my manager, Gary Moore. I was also helped a lot by John Thompson, my head coach at Georgetown.

**In your opinion, who were the three top leaders in NBA history and why do you feel that way?**
Seriously, I'll say Eric Snow. I was with him for so long in my career and I saw the leader he was, firsthand. I'll also say Aaron McKie, who played with me for eight seasons in Philly. John Thompson was also a great leader. As the first African-American coach to win NCAA Men's Division 1 Championship, he had some serious hurdles to overcome.

**In your opinion, who are the top three leaders in the league today and why do you feel that way?**
Definitely, I'll say Eric Snow because of the type of person that he is. I know that nothing about him has changed just because we aren't teammates anymore. Kevin Garnett is an influential player and Larry Brown is one of the greatest coaches the league has ever seen.

**In your opinion, who are the top three leaders in the world today and why do you feel that way?**

It's hard for me to say who the best leader is alive today. I can say that history brought us some great ones like Martin Luther King, Jr. and Malcolm X. Louis Farrakhan is also a dynamic leader.

# Epilogue:

## Leading Among Giants Starts Now

So, there you have it; all the tools you need to lead high performers in your sales force, your HR department, on the plant floor, in management or the corner offices. In this book we covered how to be a fast, fluid and flexible leader – and to apply those three helpful tools directly to your team:

- **Fast**: Speed helps you respond to change quickly, effectively and with authority.

- **Fluid**: Staying fluid helps you go with the flow and not sweat the small stuff.

- **Flexible**: Flexibility helps you do something all leaders require: adapt.

We also covered additonal leadership traits such as creating a vision and sharing that vision with your team, self-confidence, and the importance of leading from the inside out.

Now, the only question left is this: Are you ready to develop and lead high performers?

If so, I encourage you to visit **www.leadhighperformers.com** and join the **Institute for Fast, Fluid and Flexible Leaders.** Here you will have the opportunity to receive our exclusive newsletters and material which includes interviews with other leadership experts from the corporate, nonprofit, and athletic world. Additionally, you will receive high performance leadership tips, enroll in leadership development online courses such as Leading High Performers 101, 102, and 103 and The Maximizing Your High Performance Intensive.

We also offer on-site leadership training workshops with me and other of my friends for your organization. Finally, we offer a teleseminar leadership series and a Leading High Performers Boot Camp.

Visit **www.leadhighperformers.com** to learn more!

# Afterword by Bishop Eddie L. Long

## Thoughts On Success

Former Green Bay Packers head coach Vince Lombardi famously said, "Winning is a habit. Unfortunately, so is losing." That quote just speaks to my spirit. It reminds me that to live a life of excellence, I have to be committed to making excellence a part of my routine. I have to foster the opportunities that are available to me and create opportunities where there seem to be none. I have to understand what the goal is, and I have to surpass every benchmark on my way to reaching that ultimate goal.

I feel like Eric eloquently explained what a leader is in this book. As I reflect upon my experience as a leader, I must echo some of Eric's sentiments as I attempt to leave you, the reader, with the understanding that successful people have some very definite things in common. While one is obviously a huge portion of grace, maybe I can lend my agreement to Eric's wisdom by reiterating a few others.

## Identifying Your Goal

It's not enough to say what it is you want to achieve. You have to do the research. What does that mean? Well, let's say you want to be a pediatrician. That's the ultimate goal in this scenario. You can't just decide that this is what you want then sit back and wait for it to happen. That's what children do. They wish upon a star and hope that their dreams come true. As an adult, you should know better.

To become a pediatrician, you have to make above average grades in high school and college. Once you've graduated with the grades and courses you need, you can check that off the list. Next, you have to take the necessary entrance examinations and earn impressive scores to get into medical school. Once you've done that, check it off the list, too. You have to apply to the schools you wish to attend, and follow all of their protocol, as well. Do you see where this is going?

There are steps along the way, and each one is vital to achieving the final goal. You can't get to the end without going through the middle. *That's why we say our steps are ordered by God – not our leaps or our jumps.* We have to hit marks along the way to the end; and, the only way to do that is to identify what those benchmarks are ahead of time.

## Understanding Limits

I think so many of us are stopped in our tracks before we take any real steps toward our destinies. We get stopped because we have no understanding of limits. Now, why would I suggest we ponder limits when we're talking about goals and leadership? I suggest this because there's something tremendous you need to receive about the concept of limits: Limits are real. They are effective. And they have everything to do with your success. Now, let's put this in perspective. I'm not saying that you should be squashed by your limits, but I'm also not saying to ignore them. In fact, I'm suggesting quite the opposite.

If you know what the limits are – the limits that have been set by your school system, the limits that have been set by your employers, the limits that have been set by your coaches – you can effectively put them down on your list of benchmarks as something to be overcome. If I know that my limit is assistant district attorney, because my county has never before had an African-American D.A., then I know that becoming the first is something I need to check off my list. Limits don't have to be a distraction. They can be your impetus. They can be the reason you work harder. They can be the next thing to scratch off your to-do list. And, as long as you don't impose any limits on your own success, limits are another step toward winning.

## Blessings Are Real

Now, with all of this talk about goal-setting and working hard, I'm sure someone will say, "Well, the Bishop didn't mention blessings!" Of course blessings are real. (If they weren't, I don't know where I'd be!) We need the grace and blessings of the Lord. But, it's equally true that success is not happenstance. You don't just stumble upon accomplishment. You earn it by believing it's possible, by practicing it and by living it – despite circumstance. The ability to have vision is God-given. He has allowed his people to see their possibilities, and has often shown them the steps to take toward become their best. The choice to walk in that vision is solely up to you. That's the reason the Word tells us, "Faith without works is dead." (James 2:20) Believing is not enough. Vision plus belief plus activity … well, there's an equation that works!

## Don't Get Stuck in the Wait

"But, I shouldn't plan my life so far out. The Bible says to wait on the Lord." That's what you were thinking, right? If you weren't, good for you! You see, don't misunderstand the Word. Isaiah 40:31 reads, "But those who wait on the Lord shall renew their strength; they shall mount up with wings like eagles, they shall run and not be weary, they shall walk and not faint." Does it say, wait on the Lord if you want to get your strength renewed? Does it say for you to sit by and see what happens? I don't think so. When you're at a restaurant, and a waitress comes over to take your order, does she sit down with you and see what comes out? No! She writes your order down. She takes it to the kitchen. She works. You may have noticed that many waiters and waitresses are now being called "servers." That's because this word more accurately explains what they are supposed to do. They serve you.

And you should serve Him. Wait on the Lord – hand and foot – and, while you wait, renew your strength! You mount up. You run. You walk. And God will manifest in your life, taking you places you never thought possible, and enabling you to bring others along with you. Now that's a leader: a servant who reaps God's blessings through understanding vision, acting upon it and bringing others along for the ride.

You are already a winner. You win every single day when you get out of bed. You win when you take a step toward your destiny. You win as you help others reach theirs. The world sets limits to what you can do. Now go prove the world wrong. Become, as I pray this book has inspired you to, a leader and a high performer. Be blessed.

# Author Bio:

# Eric Snow

Few professional athletes can be labeled with the term "community ambassador" better than Eric Snow. With a career that included three trips to the NBA Finals (1996, 2001, & 2007) the former Big Ten Defensive Player of the Year and second round pick from Michigan State University did it all on the court. Recognized as a winner on nearly every team he has ever played on, Snow was one of the few players in the league who could be called a true team leader.

In his first book *LEADING HIGH PERFORMERS* (Morgan James, December 2009), Snow discusses what corporate, non-profit, and community leaders can do to bring out the best in people -- a topic with which Eric has a unique knowledge. While he never possessed the gaudy statistics to be regularly mentioned among the league's elite point guards, Snow played with and had incredible success against many of the best NBA players. And when stars such as Gary Payton, Allen Iverson, and LeBron James are eventually inducted into the Pro Basketball Hall of Fame, each of them could easily say that it was the assists from Eric Snow on and off the court that helped make their success possible.

This is what Snow did for more than a decade in the NBA -- help others to realize their goals. And the only part of his professional life that may be able to outshine the more than 4,200 NBA assists he dished out to his teammates might be the number of other ways in which he helped the NBA by being one of its most consistent and well-known community spokespersons.

Snow has made a point of not only being a leader among his peers, but also with his neighbors. Through his Shoot for the Moon Foundation, Snow has had a tremendous influence on the lives of thousands of people, particularly men, children, and families.

Since its founding by Snow in 1997, the foundation has been dedicated to supporting and strengthening communities and families within the Philadelphia, Northeast Ohio and Greater Atlanta metropolitan regions. The foundation strives to accomplish this goal through an emphasis and concentration on community activities aimed at empowering and encouraging fathers in their relationships with their children and families. It also addresses needs in the areas of business and home ownership, the promotion of men's health and wellness, economic development, financial security, education, employment, and social policy as it relates specifically to men, fathers, and families.

Overall, the foundation has helped to raise more than $250,000 for fathers and families, provided relief for Hurricane Katrina victims, contributed aid for students in Eric's hometown of Canton, Ohio, and even covered funeral expenses for a young African American student athlete from Cleveland who lost his life and promising future to violence.

Long before Snow became an NBA star and public figure, he was receiving special attention for his leadership. As a senior at Michigan State University, he was presented with the Chester Brewer Leadership Award, which noted both his athletic as well as his academic achievements along with his strong record of exemplary character and leadership. He was one of only four Spartan basketball players ever recognized with this honor in the university's long and distinguished history. He has since been the recipient of numerous community and parenting awards from the NBA, civic organizations and national initiatives.

Now officially retired after his 14th NBA season, Snow currently resides with his wife and three children in Atlanta. During the NBA season, he serves as a studio analyst for Turner Sports' NBATV. He is also a sought-after public motivational speaker, conducts specialized basketball skills camps and clinics year round, and has a growing international telecommunications company as a 5Linx, Inc. franchise owner (www.5Linx.net/snow).

Snow and his wife DeShawn, along with their sons E.J., Darius, and Jarren, have long-term plans to remain highly involved in community organizations located in the Greater Atlanta region, and many of his long-standing outreach activities have been shifted to Atlanta.

DeShawn Snow has also been quite active with her own community vision and founded the DeShawn Snow Foundation (www.deshawnsnowfoundation.org), which focuses on empowering young mothers and girls. Eric Snow serves as a board member to this Foundation.

For more information, to see some of Eric's past and present community work or to learn more about his athletic accomplishments, please visit www.eric-snow.com.

# BUY A SHARE OF THE FUTURE IN YOUR COMMUNITY

These certificates make great holiday, graduation and birthday gifts that can be personalized with the recipient's name. The cost of one S.H.A.R.E. or one square foot is $54.17. The personalized certificate is suitable for framing and will state the number of shares purchased and the amount of each share, as well as the recipient's name. The home that you participate in "building" will last for many years and will continue to grow in value.

**Here is a sample SHARE certificate:**

## YES, I WOULD LIKE TO HELP!

*I support the work that Habitat for Humanity does and I want to be part of the excitement! As a donor, I will receive periodic updates on your construction activities but, more importantly, I know my gift will help a family in our community realize the dream of homeownership.* **I would like to SHARE in your efforts against substandard housing in my community!** *(Please print below)*

PLEASE SEND ME _____ SHARES at $54.17 EACH = $ $_____

*In Honor Of:* _____

*Occasion:* (Circle One)   HOLIDAY   BIRTHDAY   ANNIVERSARY

OTHER: _____

*Address of Recipient:* _____

*Gift From:* _____ *Donor Address:* _____

*Donor Email:* _____

**I AM ENCLOSING A CHECK FOR $ $_____ PAYABLE TO HABITAT FOR HUMANITY OR PLEASE CHARGE MY VISA OR MASTERCARD** *(CIRCLE ONE)*

Card Number _____ Expiration Date: _____

Name as it appears on Credit Card _____ Charge Amount $ _____

Signature _____

Billing Address _____

Telephone # Day _____ Eve _____

**PLEASE NOTE:** Your contribution is tax-deductible to the fullest extent allowed by law.
**Habitat for Humanity • P.O. Box 1443 • Newport News, VA 23601 • 757-596-5553**
**www.HelpHabitatforHumanity.org**